# THE CHRISTIAN VIEWS HISTORY

## Howard Grimes

Published for the Cooperative Publication Association by

 ABINGDON PRESS
Nashville and New York

THE CHRISTIAN VIEWS HISTORY, BY HOWARD GRIMES

*261.7*

*G 88 c*

*69167*

Copyright © 1969 by Abingdon Press

*March, 1970*

## The Cooperative Through-the-Week Series

This material has been developed through the cooperative efforts
of many denominations, seeking through an interdenominational
agency, the Cooperative Publication Association, to provide resources of the best possible quality.

PRINTED IN THE U.S.A.

**For Richard**
who is helping me live
in a new generation

# PREFACE

When I was invited to write this book, I accepted with both
fear and anticipation—fear because I knew the subject was a
difficult one, anticipation because I welcomed the opportunity
to work through the subject. The subject is the one which
resulted in the chapters that follow—a Christian view of history. The task came at an opportune time for me. I had been
considerably influenced by the emphasis on *holy history* in
the late 1940's and in the 1950's. Then in the 1960's, the tide
had turned so that the so-called secular theologians as well as
others began to emphasize the relation of God to all of life. I

needed to get these two emphases into some kind of relationship.

I hope that the resolution of this problem comes through in the book, for it was my chief struggle. I come away from the struggle with a continued and deep appreciation for the unique character of the Jewish-Christian heritage. On the other hand, I have been enabled to see more clearly that heritage in the broader context of God's universal concern for all mankind. If this book has a single thesis, it is this: the biblical perspective that comes to focus for the Christian in Jesus Christ enables us to see all of life and history as the arena of God's action. I have tried to make this point again and again.

So many persons have contributed to my search that I cannot begin to name them. Some are listed in the footnotes, others in the selected readings. The list could have been much longer, but I have decided that long lists of books tend to be more confusing than helpful for most people.

In addition to the written materials, specific persons have been of great aid: Dr. Frances Eastman, who directed the committee review process of the manuscript and the committee who commented on the manuscript; my editor, Mrs. Maryruth Cannon, who, among other things, helped me clarify my writing both in terms of ideas and sentence structure; my wife, Johnnie Marie Grimes, who served as a sounding board, as she has so often, for ideas and illustrations; and Mrs. Anne Norris, who typed both drafts of the manuscript and is to be commended not only for her efficient typing but also for her ability to unscramble and interpret additions and changes scribbled in my illegible writing.

Since the manuscript which I submitted proved to be too long, it was edited by Mrs. Cannon, to about two-thirds of its original length.

HOWARD GRIMES
DALLAS, TEXAS
1968

# CONTENTS

# Chapter I

# MAN
# AND
# HISTORY

Why should the average human being—a term which applies to most of us—be interested in history? Isn't history a subject to be studied in school and forgotten as soon as the course is over? Isn't its serious study something to be left to specialists? Why should the Christian be interested in history? What, if anything, can man learn from historical study, and what in particular can the Christian learn? Is there any significance in studying history as such—either general or church history—and especially is there any reason for seeking to understand the *meaning* of history?

This book is addressed to these and similar questions, with more than a passing interest in the relationship between the study and teaching of history from a Christian perspective and from other perspectives. Its purpose is to offer in summary form relevant material concerning the nature, purpose, and value of historical study; the problems and the meaning of history itself; and the help such study and understanding can give in responding to God as revealed in Jesus Christ. The special question for the concerned Christian is, What is God trying to say to us in the process of the unfolding life of the past and of the present?

## CREATURES OF HISTORY

Let us address ourselves now to a question that is basic to others related to the study of history, Why should we be concerned with history? Or, Why should we study the past?

The most obvious reason for studying history is that all of us are involved in history and in history-making. We are creatures of history. For the time being, I shall not attempt a technical definition of history, but will use the term as an equivalent for the *ongoing process of life*. To say that man is alive is to say that he is engaged in making history—that is, he is a part of a chain of events having some casual relationship.

The word *history* is used by the historian also to denote a specialized kind of inquiry into the past, and a limited number of persons are concerned with history from this point of view. The scientist *studies* the nature of the ocean, but the fish *live* in it. The historian seeks to understand history; in the meantime, all of us are part of history. In this book, we shall become historians as we try to understand the meaning of the past; but we were involved in history long before we began to study it. Since we are history-making creatures, however, we should be interested in becoming self-conscious about the historical process.

We are involved, first of all, in our own personal history and in our family history. We were born on a particular day to particular parents who themselves had been born, back to whatever family origin the genealogist might discover for us. We have a family history, which is both a biological inheritance and a socio-cultural inheritance. That is, our family did things, held ideas, and looked at life in particular ways. Even though we may have tried diligently to rid ourselves of our history because we no longer approve of it, we can never do so completely. To do so, indeed, would make us split personalities. Wholeness requires that we to some extent assimilate our history into a whole. One of the problems with which a child who is shunted from one home to another must deal is that of sorting out the bits of his history and relating them in such a manner that he develops at least a semblance of wholeness in his personal history.

We are also a part of a regional history: we share in the background of whatever geographical area is native to us and of that to which we may move. Southern Germany is quite different from northern Germany, even in language, as the northern differs from the southern United States. The conduct of both the Anglo- and Afro-American in the deep South is the result of two centuries of history, regardless of how much recent events may have modified that history. To say that this history should be transcended, as should any regional history, is to diminish neither the fact of its existence nor the problem of dealing with it.

National history is also a part of the warp and woof of existence. To be sure, one can enter into the history of a nation not his own, though it is difficult to get entirely out of a history one assimilates as a child. Immigrants to a different nation are likely to follow one of four patterns or some combination of the four. Some remain so much a part of their own culture that their move is scarcely more than geographical. Others attempt to deny their old culture entirely. For others there is constant conflict between the old and the new. Still others have achieved wholeness through a blending of the new and the old into some kind of integrated reality.

Every person is also a part of the history and culture of some major part of the world. The rift between China and Russia has come as a surprise to many people who assumed that a common ideological base in Marxism was enough to overcome the long history of conflict between the two countries. Although there are repeated attempts to find some basis for better relationships, the long history of rivalries between the two nations makes the effort extremely difficult. The two nations are victims, to the benefit of the noncommunist world, of their histories.

The philosophies which are a part of the history of East and West also make relationships between these major parts of the world difficult. As the world has been drawn more closely together, the differences have been to some extent overcome, though in other ways they have been only accentuated. Rudyard Kipling noted this some years ago when he wrote in "The Ballad of East and West,"

> Oh, East is East, and West is West, and never the twain
> shall meet,
> Till Earth and Sky stand presently at God's great Judgment Seat. . . .

Kipling's knowledge of Eastern culture, as well as his grounding in that of the West, made his statement more than a theory of cultural conflict. It is difficult, for example, for a Westerner to accept the somewhat passive attitude toward life characteristic of much Eastern thought (Indian, for example), just as it is equally difficult for the Easterner to accept the activistic nature of Western thought. Whether East and West can meet in a creative rather than a destructive manner is one of the riddles of the future.

If we are creatures of history—or more exactly, creatures of histor*ies*—then it is important that we not only recognize the fact but also seek to deal with it. Knowledge of these historical traditions, together with an understanding of the meaning of history itself, is one step in facing the traditions creatively; and understanding them is a prerequisite to dealing creatively with problems of the present.

## THE PREVALENCE OF HISTORICAL STUDY

The ancient origins of the study of history indicate its venerable position in man's thought-world. Indeed, its beginning may be traced back to tribal lore, myths and legends, and primitive song and poetry.[1] Such "prehistory history"

---

[1] I am dependent for the ideas in the next few paragraphs on James T. Shotwell, *An Introduction to the History of History* (New York: Columbia University Press, 1922) and Harry Elmer Barnes, "History: Its Rise and Development," in *Encyclopedia Americana* (New York: American Corporation, 1966), Vol. 14, pp. 205-264.

served to give identity to a tribe as the glories of its past heroes were celebrated. It served also to provide meaning for life and answers to its questions as stories of the gods developed and myths of the origin of the world, life, and man came into being.

Later, records were kept of the names of the people: the Palermo Stone indicates an early origin of such records in Egypt, dating back probably to the twenty-eighth century B.C. Such records are more common for a later period, the Old Testament chronologies being familiar examples. At first the interpretive materials—such as the myths—and the chronicles—consisting of names, dates, and deeds—seem to have been kept separate. Our Old Testament represents the bringing together of both record and interpretation; for as we shall later see, our present Old Testament records are almost always, if not always, interpreted history, or history told for a purpose.

History as the more or less scientific pursuit of truth and understanding began, at least in Western civilization, with the Greeks. Herodotus, of the fifth century B.C., is usually considered the father of historical study in the modern sense of understanding the past. Homer, more than two centuries earlier, had written of the past in terms of myth and legend. The history Herodotus wrote, divided into nine books, was the first "secular" history—that is, it was an attempt to explain the past of man in a naturalistic and realistic fashion without particular reference to the gods.

From primitive man to modern scientific man, history in one form or another has had its place in human learning. Although the emphasis today is not as much on the past as it was several centuries ago, or even a hundred years ago, man is still fascinated by why he is where he now is. Indeed, new dimensions of historical study have recently developed in such areas as the history of science and similar types of human pursuit. It may well be that, as the understanding of history advances, it will assume a greater role in human learning than it now occupies.

As we shall later see, there are understandings of history

13

which are closely related to, if they do not in fact derive from, a Hebrew and Christian understanding of life. Thus, if Western culture has been and still is concerned with the past and its interpretation (with events and their meaning), the churchman must also be interested in historical study. Another reason those of the Jewish-Christian tradition must be concerned with history, as we shall also see later, is that one of the major characteristics of that tradition is its sense of history.

## HISTORY AS GUIDE TO THE PRESENT

The writer of the Epistle to the Hebrews points to a third reason for interest in history. After calling the role of the faithful in Hebrew history, from Abel through Abraham and Moses to the prophets, he concludes:

> And what of ourselves? With all these witnesses to faith around us like a cloud, we must throw off every encumbrance, every sin to which we cling, and run with resolution the race for which we are entered. (Hebrews 12:1, *The New English Bible.*)

Although the precise meaning of the statement is not that we learn from history, it points toward the past as context for present faith. One of the reasons for studying history is for help in finding our way in the present.

Approaching history in relation to the present assumes that history is more than a record of the past. It asserts that we look at the past, interpret it, and find meaning and significance for the present. This is essentially the Christian understanding of history (or human life) as the medium for God's self-revelation. The Christian finds in God's revelation of himself in the events of history, especially his incarnation or self-dwelling in Jesus Christ, the basis for meaning today.

It is not alone the Christian who finds keys to the meaning of life in the past, however. James Harvey Robinson, a late nineteenth- and early twentieth-century historian, saw what he called the "new history" as coming "to meet our daily

14

needs." [2] Although many historians would reject this function of historical study, many others not only assert it but search the past for clues to responsible action in our time.

As one reads the history of world civilization, one is often inclined to agree with the philosopher Hegel that "peoples and governments never have learned anything from history." One can only wonder, for example, whether Anglo-Americans in the United States have really learned anything from the long record of injustice regarding Afro-Americans. To be sure, some southern cities have learned that it is economically desirable to break down the barriers of segregation. Too often, however, one set of injustices is set aside only to be replaced by another. Schools are desegregated, a neighborhood becomes a Negro ghetto, and segregation is again in existence.

The sins of injustice and idolatry against which the eighth-century Old Testament prophets poured out their criticism are repeated over and over in dress appropriate for the time in question. The self-righteousness of the scribes and the Pharisees can be observed in the self-righteousness of institutional religionists of all times, including our own.

It is more difficult to indicate examples of man's learning from history than of his failing to do so. The point here, however, is not *whether* man has learned from history, but that he *should* so learn. In fact, the Christian understanding of revelation is closely related to this aspect of historical study. As the late Richard Niebuhr, one of the most profound recent theological thinkers, put it, "Revelation means for us that part of our inner history which illuminates the rest of it and which is itself intelligible." [3]

Learning from the past, then, is not a simple matter of saying "We won't make the mistakes of the past." Hopefully, we will not repeat all of them. Learning from the past, rather, consists of saying "The insights which come to us from the past provide a guide that can illuminate the present and help us find our way. We cannot *follow* the past; we can secure help in meeting the problems of the present."

[2] From "History: Its Rise and Development," by Harry Elmer Barnes, in *Encyclopedia Americana*, Vol. 14, p. 242.

[3] From *The Meaning of Revelation*, by H. Richard Niebuhr (New York: The Macmillan Company, 1941, 1960), p. 93.

## HISTORY, WESTERN CULTURE, AND THE JEWISH-CHRISTIAN TRADITION

We turn now to a fourth reason for understanding history and studying it—namely, the historical character of the Jewish-Christian heritage in particular and of Western culture in general. We shall have occasion to return to this basic theme, the historical nature of Christian thought, repeatedly throughout the following chapters. For the present I introduce it as one of the recurring themes of the book.

The historical character of Christianity can be seen by contrasting a nature-oriented and a history-oriented life and religion. On the simplest level, we can illustrate the nature-oriented person by describing him as one who is primarily concerned with satisfying his natural desires—for food, sex, and immediate enjoyment. The history-oriented person, on the other hand, while not unconcerned with immediate physical needs, is also oriented toward his heritage and toward the future. In other words, he is concerned with history: he sees his life as a part of a process involving the past and the future as well as the present.

In spite of the fact that primitive man had a simple kind of history in his tribal lore, his life was essentially rooted in nature rather than in history. It was with the forces of nature that primitive man had chiefly to contend: cold and heat, lightning and earthquake, crop failure and destructive floods, the persistent search for food. Primitive religion was usually if not always related to the natural world, since man himself was directly dependent upon nature. If one's life depends on growing yams, as in some of the South Sea islands, a ritual is likely to develop for the planting of the yam. If a good catch of fish is essential for the preservation of the tribe, then it is not enough that there be good fishing boats; elaborate ways must be sought to manipulate the gods to insure a good catch.

Hebrew religion originally may have been closely associated with nature: even in its developed form there is much of nature in it. The Psalms (for example, Psalms 19) and Job (chapters 37-39) contain many references to the natural world, though with a distinctive point of view—namely, that

16

it is Yahweh (God) who is responsible for nature. The distinctive element in developed Hebrew religion, however, is historical, as even a casual reading of the Old Testament will make clear. It was God who had done marvelous things for man from the beginning of time. He had called unto himself a special people—first through Abraham; later through Moses. He had delivered his people from Egyptian bondage and had led them to a new land. Whatever elements of nature are in the Psalms are far overshadowed by the historical emphasis.

Psalms 136 is a good example of the balance between the emphasis on God in nature and God in history in Hebrew thought. Verses 4 through 9 describe the creative power of God, while verses 10 through 22 are concerned with his presence in the history of Israel. He brought Israel from the land of Egypt (verses 10-15), led them through the wilderness (verse 16), and made it possible for them to possess the land (verses 17-22). The recurring refrain, "for his steadfast love endures for ever," is therefore much more closely related to events of Hebrew *history* than to the glory of God in *nature*.

The struggle of Israel with her neighbors in the land of Canaan was twofold: first, to gain and keep possession of the land; and second, to maintain the worship of the God who had delivered his people from bondage. It is at the latter point that the dramatic difference between Hebrew religion and the religion of the surrounding peoples becomes clear. Canaanite religion was essentially a nature religion. The chief god was Baal, and the lesser gods were also baals. The purpose of the gods was largely to assure fertility both to the soil and to man. The conflict between Baal-worship and the worship of Yahweh was a recurring one for centuries. (See Judges 2:11-12; 1 Kings 18:20-40; and Hosea 9:10, 11:1-2 for examples in three periods of Hebrew history.)

Although the Old Testament is not often explicit about the reason for the conflict, it was partly due to the perennial temptation of the Hebrews to turn toward the gods of nature rather than to worship Yahweh. Yahweh had revealed himself in the history of the people; but that history, concerning not a settled agricultural people but a collection of nomadic

17

tribes, became increasingly remote. The growing urbanization of the people entered into the situation, as did other factors. So far as Baal worship is concerned, however, it appears to be essentially a struggle between a history-oriented and a nature-oriented religion.

As Herbert Butterfield, professor of history at Cambridge University, has summarized it,

> The God who brought his people out of the land of Egypt, out of the house of bondage, was to be celebrated in the Old Testament pre-eminently as the God of History. It seems to have been when the children of Israel lapsed into idolatry—gave themselves over to the worship of Baal, for example—that they turned rather to the God of Nature, glorifying the forces of the physical universe and the fertility of the earth. Nothing could have served better to enhance the preoccupation with history than the fact that Jehovah was bound to His people by a promise, while they themselves were admitted to be under special obligations by the terms of the Covenant that He had made with them.[4]

It is this history-oriented religion, unlike much of that in the East, that became dominant in Western culture. Although Eastern religion is not always nature oriented, it is not usually historically oriented. Much Hinduism and Buddhism, for example, share a lack of concern for the process of life in this world—for history. The goal of life is not self-fulfillment under God, but self-negation, or absorption into Nirvana, the great soul of the universe. Rebirth, or reincarnation, is a curse; union with Nirvana and the breaking of the endless round of births is life's primary goal.

Rather strangely, much Greek philosophy bears some of the same characterstics. Plato's emphasis on the Ideal in contrast with the Real world was later corrupted into Gnosticism with its denial even of the reality of the physical. This preoccupation with the timeless world in contrast with the world of time and space (that is, history), though not universal, was

---

[4] From *Christianity and History*, by Herbert Butterfield (New York: Charles Scribner's Sons, 1960) , p. 9.

common in Greek thought. Reinhold Niebuhr, in commenting on similarities of Eastern religion and Greek thought, says:

> The common characteristic in all of these approaches is that a rigorous effort is made to disassociate what is regarded as a timeless and divine element in human nature from the world of change and temporal flux. The mystical, predominantly oriental, versions seek this divine and changeless element in a level of consciousness which transcends every particularity of finite existence, including the particularity of the individual ego. The rational, predominantly western-classical, version finds the divine and immortal element in human nature primarily in the power of human reason, more specifically in man's capacity for conceptual knowledge.[5]

One cannot prove that there is a direct, causal relationship between the consciousness of the divine involvement in history and the development of a dynamic society which has led to modern scientific accomplishment and technological developments, as well as to a vision of justice and equality however poorly implemented. There is, however, to say the least, a certain logical connection. If God is really concerned with what happens in man's history, then man's response to God must be in terms of justice and love, not in terms of contemplation and inactivity. Furthermore, the drive toward active response to God could easily be transmuted into a drive toward a dynamic society which, among other characteristics, develops an advanced technology.

As Butterfield has put it, a historical religion

> asserts that eternity is brought into relation with time, and that the supra-terrestrial realm, the kingdom of the spirit, is not locked away, for it is here and now, and the two planes of existence intersect. . . . And a real drama . . . is being enacted on the stage of all human history—a real conflict between good and evil is taking place, events do matter, and something is being achieved irrespective of our apparent success or failure.[6]

[5] From *Faith and History*, by Reinhold Niebuhr (New York: Charles Scribner's Sons, 1949), p. 16.

[6] From *Christianity and History*, pp. 157-158.

19

## CONCLUSION

It is likely, perhaps certain, that the strong ethical sense of both Judaism and Christianity grew in part out of the belief in God's involvement in man's affairs. In contrast with an emphasis on nature (which is impersonal), a concern for history elicits the necessity of response to a person-regarding God. Butterfield has reminded us of an example of a modern resurgence of nature-religion in the philosophy of Adolf Hitler in Nazi Germany. Hitler and his chief "philosopher," Alfred Rosenberg, developed a kind of nature-religion as one part of the Nazi approach to life. Hitler saw nature concerned only for the development of the species. Thus he could justify, from at least quasi-religious grounds, the mass killings of the Jews and the sacrifice of other human life and could glorify the ruthlessness of the powers of the state as a prototype of the ruthlessness of nature.

Butterfield concludes, probably rightly, that a nature-oriented view of life can easily become "the facile heresy of the self-educated in a scientific age. Too easily we may think of man as merely the last of the animals and in this way arrive at verdicts which we are tempted to transpose into the world of human relations." [7]

The contrast between the nature-oriented and the history-oriented attitudes toward life and history is therefore more than an academic point. It is central in understanding the nature of Christian faith and life. Is it too much to assert, for example, that those who would remove Christian action from the world of economic life, politics, and international relations are more Canaanite than Hebrew in their understanding of religion? If the thesis that has been propounded is correct, then it appears that they are. Further, the failure of the church and churchmen to take seriously the ethical dimensions of the gospel is not just a humanitarian failure, but is, rather, a failure of basic faith. If God is really concerned with man, then man can respond to God only through love of his neighbor in concrete ways.

[7] *Ibid.*, p. 15.

## Chapter II

# EVENTS
# AND
# INTERPRETATION

History in its simplest form, as we have seen, is equivalent to the ongoing process of life, especially as that process is viewed from the vantage point of lapsed time. The simplest man as well as the most influential man is engaged in history and history-making. Each of us has his own personal history—that is, the history of all the groups that touch his life. As men have been brought closer together into one world, their history has become world history. Junior high school students today appropriately study world history because all of us are involved in the life of the whole world.

History, therefore, appears to be simple, as, on the personal level, it may be. But matters do not remain on their most elemental level; somehow they have a way of getting complicated whether we like it or not. Let us look at water as an illustration.

Water is a simple substance, consisting of two elements and existing in three familiar forms, as a liquid, a solid (ice), and a gas (steam). So long as there was a plentiful supply of water and man had not begun to analyze the composition of substances, water was taken for granted. But two kinds of activity have occurred to make water a complicated subject for modern man. Chemical analysis of water ($H_2O$) is one factor in the process, but the more significant fact is that we can no longer take water for granted. Man's very existence depends on his taking water seriously enough to insure a plentiful supply in the future.

How has this come about? For one thing, population increases and an increase in *per capita* consumption of water have caused serious drains on water supplies. The pollution of streams, the erosion of land, the misuse of underground water supplies—these and other conditions have made an adequate water supply one of the more complex and crucial problems facing modern man. Engineering is involved in providing maximum storage of surface water. Soil conservation and reforestation help in controlling run-off. Chemists must seek means for the desalinization of sea water. Law deals with water pollution, and so on.

So it is with history. The moment man began myth-making about the past, the process of history was no longer a simple matter of one generation's passing on to the next the knowledge of the tribe. When men began to reflect on the past and to record it, historical writing was born. As men began to reflect on the *meaning* of past events, a philosophy of history, however crude, came into being; for a philosophy of history is nothing more than the explanation a historian makes of his subject matter.

For the person who takes seriously the Jewish-Christian tradition, history can never be simple, since woven into the very fabric of that tradition is a reflective approach to the past. The eighth-century prophet Amos may well be called a philosopher of history, for he saw that God's past dealings with his people placed upon them the responsibility of faithfulness to God and justice to one another in the present. The early writings that helped form books such as Exodus, Joshua, Judges, and 1 and 2 Samuel also indicate the process of reflecting on the past. Because of the predominance of the interpretive elements in these books, in fact, some historians would not consider them history at all.

If history is only a chronicle of the past—a listing of who lived when and where—it *is* simple, though it may not always be easy to write because of the lack of accurate records. If, on the other hand, history is more than a mere chronicling of events, it begins to take on a complex character to the degree that interpretation enters into the process of writing history. Since there are different answers given to this question, it is the first we must consider as we begin to explore a Christian view of history.

## IS HISTORY OBJECTIVE?

Stated as a question, the issue with which we are to deal in this chapter is as follows: Is history a factual record of events and nothing else? Or is history at least in part an interpretation of events? Is it completely objective (that is, concerned with facts) or primarily subjective (concerned with responses to events)? On the simplest level, we may ask (and for the moment not answer) the question: What happens when two people report on a fight between a member of their own ethnic group and that of another? Do they make identical or different reports of the incident?

This issue is not just an academic one—that is, the concern only of professional historians. One of the crucial questions facing the present-day Christian as he interprets the Bible is how he will understand the truth of the Bible. Some persons feel that the reliability of the Bible depends solely, or at least substantially, on the accuracy of the historical records it contains. Others are not nearly so concerned with the historicity of these records as they are with their meaning. These two points of view represent two understandings of history, with which we are concerned in this chapter.

Not only biblical history is concerned in this issue. Many general historians insist that history can be written and taught in a purely objective way. They believe that interpretation— that of the immediate writer, of another writer on whom he depends, or of a witness to the events considered—need not enter into the telling of what happened. The question is whether two writers, starting from the same evidence, will— or even can—come out with the same history. Or to put it another way, is it possible for the writing of history to be an exact science? Can that writing be done in an objective manner?

One group of historians who answered this question affirmatively were the positivists, whose influence began in the eighteenth century and has extended into the twentieth. They believed that the task of the historian is to show what really happened. The British historian Lord Acton, editor of *The Cambridge Modern History*, reported to the Cambridge University Press in 1896 with this view in mind. We cannot yet write ultimate history, he said; but we can dispose of conventional history "now that all information is within reach, and every problem has become capable of solution." [1]

Although many historians have believed like Lord Acton that a final history, absolutely true to the facts, might eventually be written, others have questioned his assumption. Sixty years after Lord Acton made his statement, Sir George Clark, in the introduction to the second *Cambridge Modern History*, replied to Lord Acton, concluding that "there is no 'objective' historical truth." [2]

In a similar vein, W. H. Walsh, in *Philosophy of History: An Introduction*, writes that "there functions in historical thinking a subjective element different from that which is to be found in scientific thinking, and . . . this factor limits, or alters the character of, the objectivity which historians can hope to attain." [3] Included in the factors which cause a his-

[1] Quoted in *What Is History*, by E. H. Carr (London: Macmillan & Company, 1961), p. 1.
[2] Quoted in *Ibid.*, p. 2.
[3] From *Philosophy of History: An Introduction*, by W. H. Walsh (Harper Torch Book, 1951, 1960), p. 98.

torian to look at the past from a particular point of view, Walsh says, are the following.

First, the facts with which a historian deals condition how he will write history. For one historian, it may be quite important that Queen Elizabeth I did much in the shaping of the Church of England, while another historian will largely ignore this aspect of her reign. In fact, whether one calls her Elizabeth I and the present Queen, Elizabeth II, depends on whether one is English or Scottish. The pure Scotsman, over whom the first Elizabeth did not reign, may refuse to call the second Elizabeth Queen Elizabeth II.

Second, a historian's personal bias will affect his writing of history. Suppose Historian A does not like George Washington, while Historian B does. Their interpretations of Washington will be colored by their personal likes or biases. Even if Historian A recognizes his bias and seeks to compensate for it in writing or teaching American history, his work will be flavored by his point of view. If he tries especially hard to be fair, he may, in fact, be subject to a reverse kind of reaction in which, as we say colloquially, he "bends over backwards" to be fair and thereby colors what he says.

Third, group prejudice enters into historical judgments. Indeed, as Walsh points out, group feelings are more difficult to deal with than personal ones; for "assumptions we make as members of a group are less easy to detect and therefore to correct than our personal likes and dislikes" (page 101). For example, Protestants are likely to be relatively unobjective in their favorable interpretation of Martin Luther, since their heritage owes much to him. For centuries, however, Roman Catholics have shared in their church's natural reluctance to see Luther as anyone other than a disrupter of the church or worse, their judgments being greatly influenced by writers who lived not long after Luther and who wrote with particular vehemence concerning his shortcomings. It has taken a great deal of effort, and considerable courage, for a new appraisal to take place by Roman Catholic scholars.

Conflicting theories of historical interpretation, or causation, are a fourth factor in how one judges historical events. For example, if one believes, as Marx did, that history is the result of economic (or materialistic) factors, one will write quite a different history of the West than if he believes in the reality of God and man's response to God as a datum of history. Similarly, if one believes that every physical act has an explanation, he will find it difficult to accept what is traditionally called "miracle," unless, of course, he also believes, as many people do, that God can and does set aside the working of these physical laws. (It might be noted that the biblical writers did not believe that God sets aside natural law, for they had no concept of natural causation. Therefore, they had no problem with the occurrences which scientific man sees as inconsistent with what he knows about the laws of causation.)

A fifth consideration in the teaching or writing of history is what Walsh calls "underlying philosophical conflicts." How will historians interpret the place of Winston Churchill in twentieth-century Great Britain? If they believe that individuals shape events to any extent, they will interpret his place in recent history differently than they will if they believe that events shape men. Since both of these poles of interpretation are somewhat extreme, perhaps most historians will see the interplay of individual and event, an interplay which involves personal judgment.

## HISTORICAL SKEPTICISM

A recognition of these subjective factors in understanding the past has led some historians to the position, bordering on historical skepticism, that accurate knowledge about the past just is not possible. Indeed, when an additional factor contributing to the problem of historical knowledge is added—namely, both the deliberate and accidental inaccuracies that have crept into historical writing—one can easily succumb to such skepticism.

A case in point is the publication of William Manchester's *Death of a President* in 1967, which contained information just as vigorously denied by the participants in the events of November 22, 1963, as it was affirmed by Mr. Manchester. Indeed, the uncertainties and disagreements concerning the assassination of President Kennedy are a living illustration of the problem of coming to accurate historical judgments. One often hears the comment, justified or not, concerning the assassination, that "we shall never know what *really* happened." This is a kind of historical skepticism.

A related, further complicating, question has to do with the vantage point from which one surveys history. Should one attempt as much as possible to view a past event as a person contemporary to the event might have seen it? Or does one judge the past by the present? If I must, in order to understand Paul's writings, for example, try to believe, as he did, that the air is literally filled with various kinds of evil spirits, I face an impossible task; and some degree of historical skepticism seems inevitable. If we must divest ourselves of our present modes of thinking, we may experience such a discontinuity between past and present that we can really gain no understanding of the past at all.

It would appear, then, that we must look at the past from our own vantage point if we are to arrive at any significant understanding of the past. As one contemporary theologian and contributor to historical understanding, Van Harvey, puts it, "the warrants and the backings for historical judgments lie grounded in present knowledge." [4] Harvey's conclusion is not that historians can be "accurate"—and certainly not infallible —but, rather, that they can be responsible in assessing the past even though their interpretation of the past is inevitably colored by the way they look at life today.

## RESPONSIBILITY IN HISTORIZING

The question whether historical judgments can be reasonably responsible is not merely an academic one, to be left to the scholar alone. The nonscholar ought also to be sensitive as he reads any book that deals with events in either the recent or remote past. The reader constantly should ask of the historian the following questions: What are your sources? Have you checked these sources against others? What is your bias,

[4] From *The Historian and the Believer*, by Van A. Harvey (New York: The Macmillan Company, 1966), p. 71.

as a person or as a member of a group? What assumptions have you made, either deliberately or unconsciously, as you interpreted facts and events? Further, the reader or hearer must ask himself: From what perspective does the speaker or writer speak or write? What is his academic background? What axes does he have to grind? What is he trying to prove? Is he dealing responsibly with facts and events, or is he using them to prove his point?

Extremist writers of all varieties, for example, are notoriously lax in their checking of sources. Charges of disloyalty are often brought to bear on innocent people because some person failed to assess his sources and to check them for accuracy. An even more obvious fault is the failure to give sources. In trying to trace an accusation brought against some person to the effect that he is "subversive," one often finds it next to impossible to ascertain what the extremist writer really means by subversion. Even when this meaning is discernible, however, it is then next to impossible in many instances to find any source cited, much less a reliable one. Often one writer has simply followed the mistakes of a former one without in any sense checking to see if the original writer knew whereof he spoke.[5]

To put the matter in other terms, there *is* a difference between history and propaganda. The propagandist chooses those ideas which serve his purpose, condemns by innuendo, or deliberately misrepresents the facts. The historian, though he cannot eliminate his subjective bias, nevertheless makes a serious effort to be fair to all aspects of his concern.

Historical writing and teaching can be done responsibly, even if it cannot be done with complete objectivity. Most of us have played the old game of "Gossip." The first person whispers a sentence to the next person, the second person repeats what he has heard to the third, and so on around the circle. Often the last person repeats to the entire group something quite opposite from the original statement.

Suppose, however, that the first person writes out his state-

---

[5] An invaluable source of help in understanding this problem is the monthly paper *Homefront*, published by the Institute for American Democracy, 1330 Massachusetts Avenue, N.W., Washington, D.C. 20005.

ment so that everyone can read it. He provides opportunity for questions, and even explains the meaning of words he uses. The process of selective perception still will be operating in each person who reads the statement and hears the discussion, and there may still be differing interpretations of the process. But the methodology employed has been responsible, and there is at least a greater chance that some agreement on what has taken place will result.

## THE "PERSPECTIVE" VIEW OF HISTORY

Although we shall have occasion under many circumstances to consider the meaning of the "perspective" view of history, a brief comment on it is needed at this time. Briefly, this view insists that history is inevitably viewed from a particular point of view or perspective. This is the understanding of history we have been considering thus far. Now we must note the differing degrees to which one depends upon and justifies his particular perspective on the past.

At one extreme, as noted above, is the propagandist, who deliberately *uses* historical data to get over his point. Somewhere near the propagandist, but with a very different motive, is the historian who adheres to what Van Harvey calls "hard perspectivism." Unlike the propagandist, a responsible historian following the line of hard perspectivism freely admits his perspective, but sees little if any reason to attempt to discern the "raw" nature of the historical data with which he deals.

Applied to Old Testament study, such a view leads to a lack of concern for "what really happened" in the history of Israel. All that matters is the interpretation given by Israel to the events in her history. Some scholars conclude that it is not possible to arrive at anything like a realistic view of the events, since event and interpretation are so closely interwoven that nothing short of new sources clearly pointing to the same event could separate the two. Nor would it really help faith if the two could be clarified.

A modified perspectivism is found in the interpretation of Jesus Christ by contemporary New Testament scholar John

Knox. Knox frankly and with no great sense of loss insists that it is impossible to separate event and interpretation in the New Testament, that what we have there with regard to Jesus Christ is a historical person mediated through the eyes and ears of the early church. It is "event plus interpretation," and both are seen as a means of God's self-revelation.[6]

Although Harvey raises questions about the extreme perspectivist, he does not deny the necessity of what he calls "soft perspectivism." This approach recognizes that everyone has a perspective. Soft perspectivism does not, however, relegate the historical task to a place of unimportance, but insists that it *is* important to attempt to understand the facts of history, though it is not possible to view them without making some interpretation.

The assassination of President Kennedy, although it has been used over and over to illustrate many things, remains the event in our recent past that perhaps best illustrates how differences in perspective influence interpretations of history. For the immediate family of President Kennedy, the personal loss and grief must have overshadowed all other meanings, at least immediately following the event. It is scarcely more than a matter of speculation as to what meaning the event will have in later years. What, for example, will it mean to the life of his young daughter and son? What will they see in the event?

Official responses to the event were various. Some saw it as an occasion for examining the character of Dallas, or, on a larger scale, of the nation itself. Texas governor John Connally, himself barely spared from death, replied to the question concerning his views of why he was not killed by the same assassin that

> . . . the President of the United States, as a result of this great tragedy, has been asked to do something in death that he couldn't do in life—and that is to so shock and

[6] See "On the Meaning of Christ," in *Jesus, Lord and Christ*, by John Knox (New York: Harper & Brothers, 1947, 1958), especially pp. 214 ff.

so stun the nation, the people and the world of what's
happening to us—of the cancerous growth that's been
permitted to expand and enlarge itself upon the community and the society in which we live that breeds
the hatred, the bigotry, the intolerance and indifference,
the lawlessness that is, I think, an outward manifestation
of what occurred here in Dallas. . . .'

This extended consideration of the relation of event and
interpretation to the understanding of Christian faith is of
twofold importance. Although Christianity is a historical faith,
its validity is not dependent upon the completely objective
reporting of past events. To make faith contingent upon the
literal accuracy of biblical history would be credulity, not
faith. Faith sees beyond facts to meaning. Faith is what happens to a person as he experiences life or when he later
responds to past events with meaning. The historical task of
the Christian is not alone to reconstruct the past; it is to see
the meaning of the past *and the present.*

The second point is that there are inevitable differences
between history as interpreted by the Christian and history as
interpreted by the non-Christian. We shall examine this point
in much greater detail later on.

## INNER AND OUTER HISTORY

Another way of deaing with the issue central to this chapter—namely, whether history can be objective—is to contrast
inner and outer (or external) history. Although we shall have
more to say in later chapters directly related to this distinction,
it must be briefly considered at this time.

The terms *inner* and *outer history* come from twentieth-
century theologian Richard Niebuhr. They are related to his
understanding that all knowledge, including historical knowledge, is conditioned by the perspective of the knower. This is
not, according to Niebuhr, a resort to skepticism nor to an
intolerably nebulous relativism. Rather, it is to assert man's

' From The New York *Times,* an interview with Martin Agronsky,
November 28, 1963, p. 23. Reprinted by permission.

incomplete perspective on all things. Otherwise, man's claims to absolute knowledge becomes idolatrous, for they tend to be substituted for the living God himself.[8]

External, or outer, history, then, is history in which I am a disinterested observer; internal history is my own, that in which I participate personally, which affects me personally, and which gives meaning to my life. It is the setting of revelation, for through it I apprehend the reality of God as he becomes "thou" to me, rather than "it." So long as he is only "it," he is an object of my interest but is not related to me personally.

Niebuhr illustrates the different qualities of these two types of history by contrasting two references to the signing of the American Declaration of Independence.[9] Lincoln's Gettysburg Address begins with a reference to the Declaration: "Fourscore and seven years ago our fathers brought forth upon this continent a new nation, conceived in liberty and dedicated to the proposition that all men are created free and equal." This is a judgment of internal history; it is an event interpreted with deep emotion by Mr. Lincoln as he points to its relation to the Civil War.

*The Cambridge Modern History* describes the same event in these words:

> July 4, 1776, Congress passed the resolution which made the colonies independent communities, issuing at the same time the well-known Declaration of Independence. If we regard the Declaration as the assertion of an abstract political theory, criticism and condemnation are easy. It sets out with a general proposition so vague as to be practically useless. The doctrine of the equality of men, unless it be qualified and conditioned by full reference to special circumstance, is either a barren truism or a delusion.[10]

[8] See *The Meaning of Revelation*, Chapter 1.

[9] See *ibid.*, p. 60.

[10] From "The Quarrel With Great Britain," by John A. Doyle, in *The Cambridge Modern History*, eds. A. W. Ward, G. W. Prothero, and Stanley Leathes (New York: The Macmillan Company, 1903), Vol. VII, p. 174.

Thus we have history seen externally, as something to be analyzed and interpreted objectively. No doubt the judgment of the passage is valid unless one interprets the event as part of a drama that gave birth to and formed the ethos for an emerging nation.

The significance for the Jewish-Christian tradition of the emphasis on inner history can hardly be missed. History is the arena of God's revelation of himself both in Israel and in Jesus Christ. If that history is viewed externally, it really is not particularly exciting. A small nation, insignificant among the nations of the area we now call the Near East, could hardly at the time have been thought of as providing the basis for Western religion and much that is inherent in Western civilization. But for those participating in the events with perception and especially for later generations, including our own, who view this history internally, it takes on a different significance.

In the same way, revelation, or God's making himself known to man, cannot be separated from a view of history that sees it as the medium by which my own life is illumined and given meaning. My interest as a Christian is not to *prove* a historical event, such as the crossing of the Red Sea. Rather, it is to find the meaning in this event for my life. This statement is not meant to imply that history as such is not important for the Christian faith. It is immensely important for faith that Jesus Christ lived, died, and was raised; but the particular events in his life, the precise place where he died, and the exact nature of the Resurrection are secondary to the principal meaning of the Incarnation. To come to the best possible historical formulations is important; it is more important for me to answer the question, What does God in Christ mean to *my* life?

## CONCLUSION

Let us now return to our original question, Is history objective? The answer that has been given is that it probably cannot be, nor is it even desirable that it be, completely objective. This does not mean, however, that the historian *as* historian is not responsible for using the best methods possible in producing an accurate, dependable history. So with the teacher of history, whether he be teaching general or church history. Although no historian, as writer or teacher, can attain to perfect objectivity, he must at least be honest and dependable in dealing with historical sources.

To state the matter in another way, the man of faith must not allow his faith to cause him not to use his God-given possibilities of being a good historian. Faith and history are related; for the Jewish-Christian tradition asserts that God has acted and does act in the realm of history, or in relation to man's life. But to make faith dependent upon the complete historical accuracy of a book such as the Bible or of some other agent is to make that *thing*, not God, the object of faith; and this is idolatry. Faith is a relationship to God, the gift of God, Paul would say; and it is not dependent upon the literal accuracy of historical details.

The man of faith should not be concerned primarily with the Bible *as history*, though he is much concerned with the Bible *as interpreted history;* that is, he is interested in apprehending what God said to men in the events of history, especially in what he is trying to say to us today through the history of the Jews and the early church, as well as in current history. When we seriously ask this question and begin to answer it, the Bible has become our story and the gospel has begun to speak to us *through* history, not *as* history. It is internal history—our family history—and may be the means by which our lives are changed.

The historian who is also a believer has a dual task. First, he must be the most accurate historian possible and examine with a critical eye all the problems of historical fact. He is also a man of faith, however; and, as such, he responds to that to which the events point—namely, to God's making himself known in and through the process of living, or history. We all participate in the same dual task. We must on the one hand utilize as best we can the best standards of historical study. On the other, we confess our faith in the living Lord of history, who transcends history and stands both inside and outside man's history.

Succeeding chapters are addressed to this dual task.

# Chapter III

# UNDERSTANDING HISTORY

Part of the perspective from which specific events are viewed is one's understanding of the historical process itself. How does life go on now, and how has it gone on in the past? At first glance, this question may appear to be the concern only of the philosophers of history, who make a special point of interpreting the entire historical process.

Like many subjects that appear abstruse and difficult to the nonprofessional, however, this subject has both its academic meaning and its significance for the common man. If a person believes, for example, that history has no meaning— that it is simply a series of happenings that, as Sartre concludes, lead to absurdity—then he has a philosophy of history.

If, on the other hand, he affirms that there is meaning in life and that meaning to some extent can be seen and understood in the process of history, then he has a different philosophy of history. Each of us has some understanding, whether he recognizes it or not, of the historical process.

Since every person does have some view of history and since one of the real dangers in life is persons' unexamined presuppositions, it is important that a book such as this one examine some of these theories. It is a further task of this book to evaluate these views from the perspective of Christian faith.

## IS HISTORY SELF-CONTAINED?

A basic question and one that the Christian certainly must ask about history is this: Is the meaning of history—if, indeed, history has meaning—to be found within the historical process itself; or does something—some power—beyond that process give it meaning? In other words, can one understand all there is to the historical process by interpreting it from the human dimension alone?

Let us here summarize briefly some of the views to which we are heir about the causes of human events.

In a prescientific world, men had no, or at least little, understanding of what we call *natural* causation, or the relation of natural cause and effect. Primitive man's conception of causation transcended the realm of nature. For example, he believed that demons caused illness; we know that germs and viruses are the culprits. He believed that the gods caused thunder; we know that thunder is the result of the heating of air by a flash of lightning and the ensuing expansion of the air and the sending out of a sound wave. Primitive man understood something of the necessity of soil, water, and light for growing crops; but he failed to see the correlation among proper planting, cultivation, and fertility. Much primitive religion, therefore, was concerned with the productivity of the land; and cultic practices involved various means of coaxing the gods to give good crops.

Israel shared in this understanding of how God acted.

Miracle was not the problem to the people of the Bible that it is to many moderns. All life was in a sense miraculous—the result of God's immediate and mighty power. Thus the early Hebrews understood that a special act of God had parted the waters of the Red Sea, had led them to victory over the inhabitants of Canaan, and had established them as possessors of the Promised Land. It is interesting to note, however, that the closer the writer was to the historic event, the less he interpreted the act as exclusively one of divine intervention. (See, for example, the Book of Nehemiah.)

Modern man, on the other hand, usually sees events from a much different perspective. To be sure, man is still very superstitious: our concern over the so-called "flying saucers," for example, is partly the result of our continuing fear in the presence of the unknown. Interestingly, however, most people want to find the *cause* of such UFO's: few if any are willing to view them only as an unexplainable invasion into man's cause-and-effect world.

This cause--and-effect perspective is the result of at least two factors: (1) the eighteenth-century rise of reason as the basis for interpreting life and (2) the scientific age, which accompanied and to some extent has grown out of the former movement. Among the theoretical formulations resulting from these emphases are *rationalism, empiricism,* and *positivism.* *Rationalism* is the assertion that knowledge derives from reason alone, without recourse to revelation or the insights of religion. *Empiricism* is the appeal to experience as the verification of truth. *Positivism,* a form of empiricism, insists that all true knowledge is fact, logic, or mathematics.

As applied to history, the cause-and-effect point of view means that events *can be explained* on the basis of natural or understandable causes. Much historical writing consists of just such explanations. Why did the Thirteen Colonies revolt against the king, and why did the settlers to the north (in Canada) not revolt? Why did English settlements in the new world turn out to be more stable than Spanish ones? What led to World War I? Why did Hitler arise out of the chaos of postwar Germany? Any schoolboy history is full of such causal explanations, though the explanations given in various texts do not always agree.

Professional historians have gone a step further by attempting to set up laws of history. These are attempts to universalize the idea of causation, by saying that things always happen in particular ways, given certain sets of circumstances. The best known example of this attempt is that of Arnold Toynbee, whose massive *A Study of History* attempts to study and compare all civilizations known to man and to determine the causes of their rise and fall. He sees as the cause of the rise of a civilization the existence of a *mean* or optimum challenge to a people to build a viable way of life. If the challenge is too great, they will be discouraged; if it is not strong enough, they will not be sufficiently motivated. So with the growth and decay of civilization, the law of challenge and response continues to operate.[1]

For example, the United States faces in the late twentieth century the greatest challenges of its history: namely, whether it responsibly can carry out the role of world leadership that devolved on it during and after World War II, whether it can deal with the racial crisis, and whether it can solve the problems of its cities. The question is whether American leadership is adequate to meet the challenge maturely or whether it will, as much of the population insists, continue to act as if we lived in the white-dominated, relatively isolated world of the nineteenth century. If the challenge is too great, according to Toynbee, the dissolution of American power may begin in the not-too-distant future.

There is an analogy on the personal level. A child must be challenged by a toy or he easily loses interest; if, on the other hand, a toy is too advanced, he may either lose interest or in some cases manifest neurotic symptoms of frustration. Unfortunately, world history is not as selective as a parent or a school can be in the challenges they offer to children; therefore, a nation may be called to exercise unusual ingenuity in seeking to meet the challenges of world conditions.

[1] See *Philosophy of History*, by William H. Dray (Englewood Cliffs, N.J.: Prentice-Hall, 1964), pp. 83 ff.

Most historians are somewhat more cautious in making any simple explanation of causality than they once were. The inexorable working of law, even in the world of nature, has often been replaced by the concept of probability, so that some scientists as well as philosophers posit the reality of the principle of indeterminism—that there are happenings for which specific causes cannot easily be found. That there are at least *patterns of history*—and therefore some kind of meaning in it—is fairly commonly accepted, however.

One way of describing the probabilities of history is by analogy. An example may be seen in the similarities of the situation in the United States now in regard to the Afro-American and that which existed in the eighteenth century vis-à-vis the Colonies and the mother country. In both instances there is repression of one group by another; in both there is an increasing demand for freedom as the possibilities for such freedom are realized. It is not accidental that the unrest of the Afro-American has followed some understanding of what equality can mean: as it has been demonstrated in the armed forces, in sports, and in the entertainment world; and as it has been projected through civil rights legislation and as improvement in the condition of the Afro-American has been actualized. Whether the end of the matter will be the same in the two periods of history depends upon how creatively leadership on national, state, and local levels responds to the challenge of the present situation.

But we have not answered the question, Is history self-contained? just by indicating the existence of historical probabilities or patterns. The Christian still must decide whether these probabilities are descriptions of how God works or whether they are substitutions for such descriptions. Can we, for example, discern the judgment of God in the race riots and other problems growing out of two centuries of suppression of the black American?

At this point, we must shift the question a bit, so that we no longer talk about laws or even probabilities in history, but about that which is the *basis* of history—that which makes history possible. We are concerned with what Langmead

Casserley calls that "without which there would not be any history at all."

> Theists . . . will talk of the purpose and will of God, of a providence which creates and respects but nevertheless in its own subtle way governs our freedom, so that man in history is ultimately limited and overruled not by impersonal purposes deriving from the interior, impersonal forces beneath him, but by an absolute Personality located in the realm of reality above him.[2]

Many persons will wish to assert the freedom of God to act in ways that man cannot finally analyze. Certainly the element of mystery must be maintained as a part of the explanation of the nature of God's relationship to the world and history. But the Christian will certainly affirm that God acts in and through historical probabilities as Creator, Sustainer, and principal Actor in what happens, whatever the way it may happen. The Christian sees history, therefore, as not self-contained.

## THE DIRECTION OF HISTORY

A second question we must ask about the historical process concerns its pattern or direction. In general, historians may be said to hold three basic views of history's over-all pattern. First, there are those who see history as chaotic, with no discernible pattern, no observable direction or meaning. It is, in the words of Shakespeare's Macbeth, "a tale told by an idiot, full of sound and fury, signifying nothing." A second view is the cyclical, in which history is seen repeating itself from one period to another. Finally, there is the linear, which asserts that history *is* moving. Its direction may be up (progressive) or down (regressive), or it may be neither up nor down; but it *is* moving to some end.

The question we are considering here is not solely a matter for speculation by professional historians. Indeed, anyone who thinks about history at all is likely to hold one of these views

---

[2] From *Toward a Theology of History*, by J. V. Langmead Casserley (New York: Holt, Rinehart and Winston, 1965), p. 17.

or some combination of them. Even professional historians sometimes appear to be only partly aware of some of their assumptions.

The following illustration may help to indicate that this question is not just a matter for scholars. The day I began this chapter, a headline in the daily newspaper caught my eye: "Publisher Sees History Repeated." The article, quoting from William I. Nichols, publisher of *This Week* magazine and a visitor to the city of Dallas, describes briefly the cyclical view of history, generally accepted by the Greeks.

The "essence of history" (Mr. Nichols' term) is the "classic pattern of governmental evolution from democracy to demagogy, oligarchy and dictatorship and back again." Plato and Aristotle are cited as holding to the view of an "Athenian wheel," in which each of the four kinds of government carries the seeds of its own destruction. Interestingly, as is often the case of those who hold to this view, the writer holds some hope for his own government. If, however, American democracy turns "timid, lazy or corrupt, the wheel could turn and crush us as it has so many other democracies in the past." [3]

This cyclical view of history was held almost universally by the ancients and still prevails in the East. In this view, the historical process reflects the rotations of the heavens and the seasons, and the process of repetition is timeless. "Herodotus [the father of modern history] conceives of these patterns as regulated by ineluctable *nemesis,* a law of compensation which continually restores the balance of things. Man cannot avert his doom, and the bitter sorrow of history is that he can know so much and control so little." [4] "Nothing new happens in the universe," wrote Epicurus, "if you consider the infinite time past." [5]

Although, as we shall see shortly, the Hebrew view of history was linear, the Old Testament Book of Ecclesiastes indicates

[3] From *The Dallas Morning News,* February 24, 1967, p. 8A.

[4] From *History: Sacred and Profane,* by Alan Richardson (Philadelphia: The Westminster Press, 1964) , p. 59.

[5] Quoted in *Faith and History,* by Reinhold Niebuhr, p. 40, from Fragments, 55.

something of the cyclical view of life and history. Verse 9 of Chapter 1 especially summarizes the view:

> What has been is what will be,
>   and what has been done is what will be done;
>   and there is nothing new under the sun.

So alien is this perspective to the remainder of the Old Testament, however, that one can only speculate as to how this Greek-sounding book was accepted in the Hebrew canon.

Among modern historians who hold at least a modified cyclical view of history are Oswald Spengler, author of *The Decline of West,* and Arnold Toynbee. Toynbee qualifies the cyclical view, as in a chapter in *Civilization on Trial* he answers conditionally the question, Does history repeat itself? It does, he concludes, but "the significance of this pattern of repetition lies in the scope that it gives for the work of creation to go forward." Further, Toynbee believes that history is not *doomed* to repeat itself: "it is open to us, through our own efforts, to give history, in our case, some new and unprecedented turn." [6] While civilizations may rise and fall and the historical process repeats itself, religion, he believes, continues to grow in its insights so that a mature higher religion will thus be brought to birth.[7] Toynbee's view is thus partly cyclical, partly linear.

The third of these historical patterns, the linear, is the biblical view. Basically, this view involves an understanding of history as moving and dynamic. There is in short a doctrine of the fulfillment of history, or the belief that its ultimate meaning is found in what happens at its end. For the Hebrew-Christian heritage, God fulfills history. Karl Marx borrowed this general approach, but saw the fulfillment of history as the coming of the classless society and the withering away of the state. Utopianism of all varieties finds the fulfillment of history in some golden future age. There are, in fact, many secular versions of the biblical view.

[6] From *Civilization on Trial,* by Arnold J. Toynbee (New York: Oxford University Press, 1948), pp. 38 and 39.

[7] See *ibid.,* p. 236.

The basic historical perspective for the linear view is that of the Hebrew prophets. Although the prophets are considerably less futuristic in their thinking than they are often interpreted as being, we find in them always a note not only of what God *is* doing but also of what he *will* do. They had no conception of history as the vain repetition of one cycle after another; they had, instead, a keen sense of judgment, and sometimes of fulfillment.

Increasingly in the centuries prior to the Christian era, the eschatological element—the idea of the end of history—became more prominent in Hebrew thought. The apocalyptic emphasis, including a view of society's regression to the point that God would intervene and establish his kingdom, also developed. Much of the messianic expectation in Judaism was concerned with this conception of an earthly kingdom to be established in the line of David, with God as the author and Israel as the recipient of the apocalyptic gift.

The Revelation to John is the one book in the New Testament centered in this apocalyptic interpretation of history. Much in other New Testament books (for example, Matthew 24), however, indicates the common belief of the early Christians in the imminent return of Jesus, a belief taken up into the general apocalyptic framework.

The original prophetic insight had little to do with progression or regression in history; rather, God would come in judgment and salvation to effect the fulfillment of history. In apocalyptic thought, the basic prophetic perspective was reinterpreted to include retrogression in history and the kinds of elaborate predictions represented in the New Testament book of The Revelation to John. In nineteenth- and early twentieth-century thought, on the other hand, the basic prophetic insight of God's fulfillment of history in the kingdom of God was perverted into the idea of the gradual realization of an ideal social order. Although this view has been identified with certain aspects of the biblical view of history (for example, Isaiah 2:4; Micah 4:1-4; and Luke 13:18-21), the idea of progress was basically a modern view that became conflated with the biblical one.

The modern view of progress owes its origin, or at least its major development, to social theorists like Herbert Spencer, who applied the Darwinian view of organic evolution to society and emerged with a theory of societal evolution. Based on this view, the slogan of the social gospel and the early twentieth-century missionary movement became "The Kingdom is coming," so that "Kingdom-building" was considered the normative activity of the Christian.

There is, to be sure, an eschatological element in the Bible; but such an element is concerned only with the idea that God will fulfill or complete history. One legacy of the fourth-century theologian Augustine is that he took this eschatological element seriously but adapted it to a world in which the imminent end of the world was no longer expected.

God, says Augustine, is the Lord of history now: he always has been, and he will be in the future. Augustine saw the city of man and the city of God as intermixed, but affirmed no progressive transformation of society into the kingdom of God. He did perceive the city of God as a reality now, though incompletely realized, and he believed that God in his own time would bring its full realization. Because God is sovereign, in spite of sin in the world, history has meaning and man can live in the hope of future fulfillment. The one point at which Augustine seriously erred was his tendency to identify the city of God and the church of Rome.[8]

One of the most important aspects of a Christian view of history is the conviction that history is not a meaningless cycle of repetition. Where it is going and how it arrives, as we see in Augustine's adaptation of biblical eschatology, is not the crucial question. The crucial question is whether history has direction. It is appropriate, as Toynbee does, to see historical patterns that help interpret the present—for example, certain parallels between the declining days of Rome and the present situation in the West. But this is another way of saying that all history is under both the judgment and the grace of God. Toynbee, indeed, indicates that he has drawn upon both the Greek and the Hebrew understandings of

[8] For an interpretation of Augustine's thought, see Roger L. Shinn, *Christianity and the Problem of History* (Abbott Books Edition, 1964; Scribner's edition, 1953), pp. 29-62.

history: he finds cycles in the past but looks to the future with the hope of one who believes that ultimately God transcends the historical process.

Perhaps the most common tendency of modern man is not to look upon history either as chaos or meaningless repetition, but to find its fulfillment in science. Along with this belief in science, or perhaps as a result of it, man also tends to look at both his own self-fulfillment and the fulfillment of history as a purely human enterprise. Within recent years, the so-called "secular theologians" have tended to glorify man's accomplishments sometimes at the expense of affirming his dependence on God. The biblical view, as we have seen, however, is that the fulfillment of history is subject to the action of God.

## THE PROPER SUBJECT OF HISTORY

A third question related to our understanding of history concerns its subject matter. History deals with human events, but with what *kinds* of events? If a future historian of the twentieth century were to base his history on newspaper headlines, he would interpret much of our age in terms of crime and violence. Obviously, this is not the whole of modern life; and a further reading of newspapers, largely of their inside pages, would help this mythical historian correct his perspective.

A complete history would cover all aspects of human life. Obviously no writer or teacher of history can be so inclusive; therefore some process of selection must take place. The tendency has been, especially in academic courses in history, for the political aspects of life to be exalted above all else: the names, dates, and accomplishments of rulers; the nature, cause, and course of wars; the dates, provisions, and results of political treaties. The reason for this imbalance, it can be argued, is that these larger movements shape the life and destiny of peoples. Yet there is much more to the lives of ordinary people than political intrigue, warfare, and peace treaties.

Church history is scarcely more representative with respect to the total life of the church. For years church historians have disagreed over the relative importance of doctrinal and ecclesiastical history—that is, the history of how ideas have developed in contrast with the development of the institutional aspects of the church. A good example of a combination of the two may be found in Williston Walker's *A History of the Christian Church*. William Warren Sweet, on the other hand, was relatively unconcerned with the development of ideas in American church history, focusing principally on the institutional life of the church.

These two aspects of church history are scarcely representative, however, of the total life of the church. Many questions about the life of the church through the ages virtually are unanswered, partly, of course, because no one bothered to record seemingly unimportant details of church life. The fault is also partly due to the fact that church historians generally have not dealt adequately with existing sources. How did the early church communicate its faith to children, for example? When did infant baptism become the established practice, and why did it develop in the first place? How did laymen see themselves in relation to the clergy? To be sure, most of these questions have been treated to some extent, some of them only recently. They are not usually included in the regular church histories, however, but in specialized books.

Church history has been written almost exclusively from the viewpoint of the clergy. Only within recent years—after more than nineteen centuries of church life—has a history of the laity been produced.[9] One of the major problems confronting those who undertook the writing of its various chapters was the difficulty of finding material on the nature of the laity in the church. Secondary sources were often nonexistent, and primary ones were difficult to come by.

A further illustration of this problem in historical writing is to be found in the growing number of specialized branches of history—for example, the history of science, which requires a knowledge both of science and of history. Within the area of church history, there are various subdisciplines: for example, the history of missions, of worship, of preaching, of teaching, and, more recently, of the laity.

[9] *The Layman in Christian History*, eds. Stephen Neill and Hans-Ruedi Webber (Philadelphia: The Westminster Press, 1963).

There is no easy solution to this complex problem. The point is that any person who deals with history should be aware that he is likely to be limited both in his ability to cover the whole subject matter and in the scope of his perspective. A particularly important aspect of the problem for our purposes is the difference between the approach of the church and that of the public schools to history: many public school textbooks, for example, fail to deal adequately with the place of religion in various periods of Western history. Since we shall have occasion to return to the subject in future chapters, it need not be pursued at this time.

## DOES HISTORY HAVE MEANING?

I have assumed thus far that history does in fact have meaning, an assumption most people probably make. By this I mean that, as one studies the past, he can see patterns, meaningful relationships, and emerging values. Or to put it in religious terms, he can discern, through faith, the working of God in the events of human history. So crucial is this question for the remainder of our consideration, however, that it cannot remain an unexamined presupposition, and therefore becomes our fourth major question.

In a previous age, few questions would have been raised concerning the reality of meaning in history. One writer, commenting upon the influence of Augustine on later historical writing, says: "To say that history has a meaning was to assert that the story of mankind showed continuity and unity from beginning to end, that history, as well as nature, was subject to law, divine or rational; and that either faith or reason would reveal this inherent structure." [10]

No longer can it be assumed, however, that most men discern this meaning. For some, the whole sorry affair of life is meaningless, even chaotic. More common among literary men than among professional historians, this view is found in the formlessness of modern visual art, the drama of the absurd,

[10] From *The Philosophy of History in Our Time*, ed. with an introduction by Hans Meyerhoff, "History and Philosophy: An Introductory Survey" (Doubleday Anchor Books, 1959), p. 7.

and the many works of fiction that simply begin and end.

But how is meaning to be found in history? One way is that of the philosopher who finds meaning within the processes of history. He may or may not see this meaning in relation to God, though the late eighteenth- and early nineteenth-century philosopher Hegel did. Hegel attempted to interpret the entire historical process as the unfolding of the divine Idea: that is, he explained history through a reasoned approach to reality, finding in the historical process the nature of reality itself.

Not all those who have been influenced by Hegel, of course, find the meaning of history in relation to God. Karl Marx transmuted the idealism of Hegel into the materialism of communism. Instead of finding meaning in the working out of the divine Idea in history, Marx found it in terms of the working out of economic processes. Marxism has a strong sense of history: the fulfillment of history is found in its movement toward the classless society when the state will wither away and all men will live in a utopia reached not through idealistic striving but through scientific planning.

Such speculations, especially those of Hegel, are likely to leave the majority of mankind more confused than enlightened; and there is some question as to whether even the philosopher has arrived at anything like a final understanding when he has done his best thinking. In the final analysis, therefore, we are thrown back to the theological approach to history, an approach based on faith in God, who transcends history. As Reinhold Niebuhr has put it:

> The Christian faith is the apprehension of the divine love and power which bears the whole human pilgrimage, shines through its enigmas and antinomies and is finally and definitely revealed in a drama in which suffering love gains triumph over sin and death.[11]

To put it more simply, the Christian faith asserts that the reality of God gives meaning and significance to human history, especially through its central belief that God himself has entered into this history in the man Jesus Christ.

[11] From *Faith and History*, p. 233.

Christian faith insists that, because God has entered into human history, and continues to do so, meaning must be found in and through the world which often seems chaotic and absurd, that to find basic meaning anywhere else is to deny the Incarnation. Thus, as we look at the relation of God to history in the next two chapters, we will be concerned not only with the special events through which we perceive the activity of God—that is, the life of Israel, the Incarnation, and the life of the church. We shall also be interested in the affirmation that God is the Lord of *all* of history—that, in the words of the American folk hymn, "He has the whole world in his hands."

# Chapter IV

# GOD AND "HOLY HISTORY"

The Old Testament is permeated with an unmistakable sense of Israel's special vocation and God's particular intervention in her history to make known the nature of this call. It is said in many ways, though perhaps never more clearly than by the eighth-century prophet Amos:

"You only have I known
of all the families of the earth . . ." (Amos 3:2a).

The events of Israel's history, moreover, were seen as demonstrations of Yahweh's judgment and mercy as Israel repeatedly proved untrue to her call.

This sense of vocation continues in the New Testament

affirmation of God's self-revelation to the world in Jesus Christ. Although there was conflict in the early church over the precise relationship of the new faith to that of Israel, there was never any doubt concerning the continuity of the two. (See Acts 15:1-11; Galatians 1:6 through 2:21; Romans 11:1-32; Hebrews 11.)

## INTERPRETED HISTORY

We should not be surprised to learn, therefore, that biblical history is *interpreted* history, history written from the *perspective* of Israel as God's chosen people and the church as the continuation of that special relationship. It is *interior* history, history written as *our* history. It is *confessional* history, beginning, in the words of Deuteronomy 26:5, "A wandering Aramean was my father. . . ."

More exactly, the Old Testament, including its historical sections, consists of documents of faith. The Old Testament scholar analyzes these documents and seeks to distinguish between myth (stories expressing truth that is above history), legend (remembered stories of the past), and history (interpreted events of the past).[1] All three have a common purpose—to point to God's activity.

The modern biblical interpreter who insists that the biblical record stands or falls upon its literal historical accuracy has misunderstood its intention. The biblical writers are not primarily chroniclers of the past for the sake of telling a good story—as, let us say, Sir Francis Chichester is in telling of his round-the-world voyage in *Gipsy Moth Circles the World*. Rather, they see the past in terms of its present relevance. The writers' interests are in what God has done in relation to what he is now doing.

The Bible makes no distinction between sacred and secular history. Only after Augustine did the differentiation between the sacred and the secular areas of life arise. Nor was there any serious problem of separation between the two types of

[1] For a further interpretation of these three types of writing, see *From Faith to Faith: Essays on Old Testament Literature*, by B. Davie Napier (New York: Harper & Brothers, 1955), Chapters I, II, and III.

historical thinking prior to the age of reason (the eighteenth century).

As the emphasis on rational thought became more common from the eighteenth century onward, conflict did arise between those concerned with a what-really-happened approach to past history and those who accepted some interpretation of history. The conflict was compounded because, on the one hand, the rationalists failed to recognize their own perspective as based on something other than pure reason. Men of faith, on the other hand, often did not distinguish between the right—and the responsibility—of the historian to determine facts and the faith perspective from which the facts were interpreted. If the historicity of a particular part of the Bible was questioned —let us say, the Creation stories—then too often churchmen concluded that the faith itself was being attacked.

It was at least partly in reaction to this situation that the emphasis on "holy history" (*Heilsgeschichte*) became a prominent part of twentieth-century theology. For all practical purposes, there developed in the thought of theologians such as Karl Barth and Emil Brunner a conception of two histories —"public" history, subject to investigation by historians, and a "super-history," holy, or salvation, history. This history, accessible to the eyes of faith alone, included the events of the Incarnation—the birth, life, death, and resurrection of Jesus Christ. Thus the problem of the historicity of the biblical record was solved by refusing to apply to the events of salvation history the same methods of historical study applied to general, or public, history.

Rudolf Bultmann and those theologians associated with his school of thought offered a variation on the holy-history approach. Bultmann's interpreters do not agree about how far Bultmann goes in denying the importance of history; nor are they themselves in agreement regarding the relationship of history and faith. Generally, however, this school of thought holds that an objective knowledge of the historical events of the New Testament is not really important. Rather, the faith to which the New Testament events point is the crucial matter. A person acting as historian may raise all kinds of questions about the events of the Bible, while the same person acting on faith may see in them the meaning of life because he views them as the means of God's self-revelation. Thus, while Karl Barth and Emil Brunner say that the events of holy history are to be approached in a different manner from those of public history, Bultmann and his followers tend to insist that the historical events associated with key teachings are not of crucial importance.

The debate concerning history and faith goes on, and obviously we cannot solve it here. Three comments of my own related to the previous discussion seem appropriate, however.

First, I do not wish to separate the sacred and the secular. I am aware of and would affirm the distinctive and unique perspective of the Hebrew-Christian tradition. Further, I would acknowledge and rejoice in the history of the Hebrew-Christian communities. But when one applies to sacred history means of interpretation different from those he applies to general history, he has for all practical purposes made the two radically discontinuous. The secular and the religious realms of life will then ultimately be separated. I would affirm, rather, that all history is sacred because it is under God and that all history is secular because it deals with the world of men.

Second, while I recognize the difficulty of determining historical fact, I would not underrate the importance of the historical. We need serious historical study of the Bible, even though we must consider the Bible as fundamentally a record of faith. I believe that we must accept the inevitable mixing of event and interpretation in all history as well as in the Bible and not fret too much because of the difficulty of finding what really happened. At the same time, we must recognize the difference between truth of event and truth of interpretation and the importance of freeing the historian to do the best he can to understand the events behind the interpretation.

A simple illustration will help clarify this issue. I cannot remember all the details of my life with my parental family. Certain facts are known—the year I was born, what doctor was present (since he is listed on my birth certificate), how many brothers and sisters I had, where I grew up and went to school and church, when I left home. Most of these facts are incidental, however, to the most important items in my childhood and youth. Those matters are not easy to chronicle even when I remember them: the atmosphere of faith and love, the tensions as well as the reconciliations, the fears as well as the security. Were I to write an autobiography, I suppose I would give the details of my life, for they are a framework on which more meaningful ideas are hung. If I write them, I ought to report them as accurately as I can. But the details on which I can be exact are, by and large, relatively unimportant in telling others who I am and what my life is like.

The point is that the process of interpreting a life or an event inevitably leads one beyond the merely factual; and if the reporting occurs years or even centuries after the events of concern, there is no hope of being accurate in the factual sense of the word.

My third point follows from the second: the faith of the reader, as well as that of the writer, is a key in interpreting biblical history. A lack of faith on the part of the reader means, for example, that the event of Jesus Christ remains external history and nothing more. The presence of faith, on the other hand, means that the event has become internal history for him. Thus in one sense he has ceased, at least for the moment, to be historian and has become man of faith. I do not mean that a man of faith cannot also be a historian; it is simply that two different sides of his person are in operation in carrying on these two forms of activity. As man of faith, he utilizes the criteria of faith; as historian, he employs the standards of historical study.

I am aware that I have left many questions unanswered and that I have left myself open to questions from many different points of view. The problems are far too complex to treat definitively in this space. The major point I would make is that we are not concerned here only with the history of the Jewish people or of the early church, but, rather, with understanding the faith of Israel and the early church in relationship to the *meaning* of history. I see no alternative except for us to seek to understand as best we can and then accept the biblical perspective on life and history if we are to claim to be Christian. We cannot, nor do we need to, answer all of the questions the historian rightly raises about the past. Our primary task is to understand the perspective from which the Bible views life and history and to be clear whether this perspective is the one from which we view life and history also.

## THE IDEA OF COVENANT

As we examine biblical religion and its relation to history, we soon discover that the idea of the Covenant is central if not definitive. Although there is no single view of the Covenant in the Bible, certain crucial meanings of the term may be summarized.[2] One of the most important of these regards the initiator of the Covenant: It is Yahweh, not man, who initiates. "I am the Lord your God, who brought you out of the land of Egypt, out of the house of bondage. You shall have no other gods before me" (Exodus 20:2-3). Though there *is* a kind of mutuality in the Covenant, it is not between equals.

Second, the Covenant is related to history, not to nature; to deliverance from bondage through a historical event, not to the promise of fertility in herds or crops.

Third, it is a relationship freely offered by Yahweh, not one Israel has earned or deserves. Although the idea of unmerited favor (grace) is much more fully developed by the later prophets, it is evident even in the earlier documents relating to the covenant idea. By the time of Deuteronomy (seventh century B.C.), the idea of a covenant of steadfast love is made clear: The Covenant is not because Israel was mighty in number but "because the Lord loves you, and is keeping the oath which he swore to your fathers, that the Lord has brought you out with a mighty hand, and redeemed you from the house of bondage . . ." (Deuteronomy 7:8).

Fourth, once God has chosen Israel, something is expected from his people. Because Yahweh had brought Israel out of the house of bondage, Israel was to keep the commandments (Exodus 20:2 ff). In the later interpretations, such as that

[2] See "The History of the Religion of Israel," by James Muilenburg, in *The Interpreter's Bible* (Nashville: Abingdon Press, 1952), Vol. I, pp. 299-300; and *From Faith to Faith: Essays on Old Testament Literature,* by B. Davie Napier, pp. 61 ff.

found in Deuteronomy and in the prophets, the sense of obligation is even clearer. Indeed, the idea of "keeping covenant" is the basis for the strong ethical idealism of the prophets.

The covenant idea also became the basis for the legalism, seen in its beginning stages in the Pentateuch but found especially in Ezra and Nehemiah and in Jewish thought just prior to the Christian era. It is seen also in the ceremonial interpretation of Temple worship, an approach to religion which Amos, among others, thoroughly rejected. (See, for example, Amos 5:21-23.)

For these reasons, perhaps, the earlier prophets seldom use the word *covenant,* though their writings are based squarely on the covenant idea. Later prophets rescued the word and spoke of the new covenant God would make (Jeremiah 31:31-32), as well as the renewing of the Covenant (Isaiah 55:3; 61:8). In these cases, as Wright observes, "there is no longer any question about the nature of the covenant as an external, legal compact. It is based upon the pure grace of God which shall create in man a new heart and new spirit to receive it." [3] In the New Testament the word is not often used; but the idea is central, and we rightly designate these books as belonging to the New Covenant (or Testament).

## THE HISTORY OF THE COVENANT

We are on much less secure ground in relation to the origin of the covenant idea than we are regarding its centrality in biblical history. The Priestly document, one of the sources of Genesis, indicates that a covenant existed far back beyond Abraham, with Noah: "Then God said to Noah and to his sons with him, 'Behold, I establish my covenant with you and your descendants after you . . .'" (Genesis 9:8-9). The idea is much clearer in the stories concerning Abraham. Israel, as later records indicate (for example, Nehemiah 9:7-8 and Hebrews 11:8-19), saw her beginning as a people in the call of Abraham. Although Abraham was the father of the Hebrew people, he was to be one through whom "all the families of the earth will bless themselves" (Genesis 12:3).

[3] From "The Faith of Israel," by G. Ernest Wright, in *The Interpreter's Bible,* Vol. I, p. 355.

It was with Moses, however, that the covenant faith came to its full expression, just as the story of Israel begins in earnest with him. The significance of the events associated with the deliverance from Egypt—and thus with Moses—is indicated by the centrality of the Passover, the commemoration of Israel's deliverance from bondage, in Jewish life. When the Covenant is renewed under Joshua, there is some mention of Abraham (Joshua 24:2-3), but the primary emphasis is on Moses and the deliverance from Egypt (24:5-7, 16-18).

The same emphasis is found in the renewing of the Covenant after the Babylonian captivity (Nehemiah 9:7-8, for Abraham; 9:9-21, for Moses and the events associated with his leadership). By and large, the Psalms are not historically oriented, though by far the bulk of historical material refers to the events related to Egypt and those that followed.[4]

Similarly, the prophets are more concerned with the Egyptian deliverance than with Abraham's venture of faith. Four examples will serve to illustrate this fact. Three are from eighth-century prophets, prior to the Josiah reform that probably produced Deuteronomy.

> "Also I brought you up out of the land of Egypt,
>     and led you forty years in the wilderness,
>     to possess the land of the Amorite." (Amos 2:10)

> When Israel was a child, I loved him,
>     and out of Egypt I called my son. (Hosea 11:1)

> "For I brought you up from the land of Egypt,
>     and redeemed you from the house of bondage;
>     and I sent before you Moses, Aaron, and Miriam."
>                                     (Micah 6:4)

The final quotation is from Jeremiah, a contemporary of Josiah and his reform movement, Jeremiah's work reflecting some of the ideas also found in Deuteronomy.

---

[4] For example, Psalms 105:9 mentions specifically the covenant with Abraham. Among those referring in some way to the deliverance from Egypt are Psalms 68, 77, 78, 80, 81, 95, 99, 103, 105, 106, and 114.

> "For I solemnly warned your fathers when I brought
> them up out of the land of Egypt, warning them per-
> sistently, even to this day, saying, Obey my voice."
> (Jeremiah 11:7; see also 7:21-26.)

Deuteronomy 26:5-9, a ritual for the presentation of the
firstfruits at the altar, indicates the relative importance of the
Abrahamic and the Mosaic covenants. If there is any mention
of Abraham, it is the opening sentence, "A wandering
Aramean was my father. . . ." [5] The events of Egypt, on the
other hand, are noted in the remainder of the passage.

Indeed, there are deep parallels between the captivity, deliverance, and new life in Canaan, and the Crucifixion, Resurrection, and new life through Jesus Christ. It is probably not
without significance that the Crucifixion occurred at the time
of the Passover. The covenant through Moses had brought
new life to Israel. The covenant through Jesus Christ brought
new life, or at least the possibility of it, to all mankind. The
historical events Passover and Crucifixion are given meaning
and significance through the faith of those who continue to
participate in them as living realities.

## COVENANT AND HISTORY

How are we to interpret the covenant idea in relation to the
history first of Israel and then of the church? There are two
dimensions to this meaning: One is the historical in relation to
the past; the other, the historical in its relation to the present.

The entire Bible contains a strong sense of God's having
acted in the past. We have already seen how the sense of God's
prior action pervades the Old Testament. The prophets were
always calling Israel back to the past, regardless of how contemporary they might otherwise be.

The other dimension of the covenant idea is found in a
vivid sense of the living, contemporary presence of God. As
we have already noted, the prophets seldom use the word
*covenant* itself. Indeed, Napier points out that not once do

---

[5] Whether the "wandering Aramean" was Abraham or Jacob-Israel is
difficult to determine. Both Abraham and Jacob-Israel are described
as going to Egypt.

the eighth-century prophets use the word *berith* (covenant) in a passage of undisputed authenticity for the covenant between Israel and Yahweh.[6] Perhaps the prophets wished to remind the people that God's relationship to man is not just something that occurred but, rather, is something that *occurs*.

The Covenant was kept up-to-date officially in the renewing of the Covenant, as in its renewal under Joshua at Shechem (Joshua 24). The call of the eighth-century prophets, although not words of Covenant renewal, must be understood as having this meaning. The Book of Deuteronomy, probably coming out of the Josiah reform of 621 B.C., is itself the renewal of the Covenant. In Deuteronomy the tradition of Exodus is not just repeated: it is made meaningful to seventh-century Israel.

Reference has already been made to the renewal of the Covenant under Ezra, as recorded in Nehemiah. Although this redaction of the Covenant marks a rigid separation of Jew from non-Jew and the beginning of a strict legalism, it was an effort at updating the Covenant. (See Nehemiah 9, 10, and 13.) Although we can from our post–New Testament perspective denote what was happening in the growing legalism of the late fifth century onward, we must remember that, for the Jew, faithfulness to the Covenant was interpreted as keeping Torah, or Law.

The prophets saw beyond this legalism, however, and Jeremiah dreamed of the time when there would be a new covenant with the law within man's heart (Jeremiah 31:31-34). The ideas of the post-Exilic Isaiah are near to much that we identify distinctly as the new covenant. The identification of Jesus with the suffering servant of Isaiah 42 through 53 separated him from the messianic expectation of an earthly king and identified him with the emphasis on servanthood.

The life, death, and resurrection of Jesus Christ are, in their historic orientation, God's renewing of the Covenant, or, more exactly, the making of a new one. Jesus was aware of his dependence on the past and indicated that he had come

---

[6] See *From Faith to Faith: Essays on Old Testament Literature*, by B. Davie Napier, pp. 175-176.

not to abolish the law and the prophets but to fulfill them (Matthew 5:17-20). But he also indicated that the new wine could not be contained in the old wineskins (Matthew 9:17). The new forms that arose in spite of the resistance of some of the Jewish Christians indicate the newness of the covenant that centered in Jesus of Nazareth.

The Epistle to the Hebrews, perhaps the most Jewish of all New Testament books in its thought forms, picks up Jeremiah's idea of the new covenant and follows the Jeremiah passage with these words: "Therefore he is the mediator of a new covenant . . ." (Hebrews 9:15a). Although the other New Testament writers seldom use the word *covenant*, the idea is inherent in much they write. Paul, perhaps understandably, appeals to Abraham as a man of faith more fully than he does to Moses (Romans 4:1-25). But his sense of continuity between Israel and the church was keen, a fact especially illustrated as he wrestles with the problem of the relationship between the old Isreal and the new (the church). (See Romans 2 through 4, 9 through 11.)

Paul understood the importance of holding in tension both the historical and the contemporary approaches to the Covenant. Although he seldom refers to the historic Jesus, his writing reflects a keen sense of what had happened in the immediate past through Jesus as well as in the more remote past of Israel. Note these interesting and significant juxtapositions of the past and the contemporary: "While we were yet helpless, at the right time Christ died for the ungodly" (Romans 5:6). But *"we* were buried therefore with him by baptism into death, so that as Christ was raised from the dead by the glory of the Father, *we too might walk in newness of life"* (Romans 6:4; italics mine).

For the prophets and Paul, and for most if not all of the New Testament writers, the Covenant is a living relationship, not a relic from the past. It is important as we seek to understand the historic nature of the Christian faith to comprehend the reality of this point of view; for throughout the history of the church, as of Judaism, the temptation has been for men to claim the benefits, without accepting the obligations, of past action.

The covenant idea provides an unusually fruitful basis for the proper relating of historic and contemporary. The heart of the covenant idea is that God *has* entered into relationship with his people and that he *continues* to do so.

## THE QUESTION OF ELECTION

One cannot consider the matter of a covenant people without becoming involved in the notion of election or chosenness. What is the particular meaning of the history of Israel and that of the church in relation to mankind generally? Is covenant history an exclusive history, or does it have implications for all of mankind? These are only a few of the questions related to the idea of election.

There have been, in fact, two concurrent understandings regarding the consequences of being chosen. The more popular has been that election does convey special privilege. Prosperity, freedom from disease, victory over enemies—all are promised if Israel obeys the commandments of Yahweh. (See Deuteronomy 7:12-16.) On the other hand, the people will perish like the other nations if they fail to obey (8:20). It is only a step from this ethical interpretation of covenant to one which admittedly is a perversion—namely, that the chosen ones are superior and not subject to judgment.

At its best, however, the Covenant was interpreted as bringing not special privilege but special responsibility. Abraham is to be the instrument of God's blessing (Genesis 12:1-3). The Mosaic covenant is made at Yahweh's initiative, but Israel is to respond by faithfulness (Exodus 20:3) and by keeping the law (Exodus 20:4 ff). At the renewal of the Covenant under Joshua, Joshua says, "You are witnesses *against yourselves* that you have chosen the Lord, to serve him" (Joshua 24:22; italics mine). Amos says quite trenchantly:

> Hear this word that the Lord has spoken against you, O
> people of Israel, against the whole family which I
> brought up out of the land of Egypt:
> "You only have I known
>    of all the families of the earth;

61

> therefore I will punish you
> for all your iniquities." (Amos 3:1-2)

The post-Exilic writer of the last part of Isaiah further expands the notion of covenant and accountability:

> "I am the Lord, I have called you in righteousness,
> I have taken you by the hand and kept you;
> I have given you as a covenant to the people,
> a light to the nations,
> to open the eyes that are blind,
> to bring out the prisoners from the dungeon,
> from the prison those who sit in darkness."
>
> (Isaiah 42:6-7)

Although the terminology of the New Testament is not the same, the idea remains. Jesus' conception of his ministry was as servant: ". . . I am among you as one who serves" (Luke 22:27; see also Luke 4:18-19). The messianic figure that emerges from the Gospels is not that of the triumphant king, but rather of the suffering servant.

Not only must the idea of election be seen in relation to this call to special responsibility; it must also be related to the incipient and at times explicit universalism of the Bible. Abraham is to be the one through whom *all* the families of the earth are to be blessed (Genesis 12:3). Amos is concerned not only with the sins of Israel and Judah (the northern and southern kingdoms), but also of the surrounding nations (Amos 1:3 through 2:3). Cyrus the Persian is God's anointed (Isaiah 45:1). The writings of the post-Exilic Isaiah are saturated with the idea of the servant (probably Israel) whose mission is to serve others. (See, for example, Isaiah 42:1-9; 53.)

Jonah is commanded to go to the "heathen" city of Nineveh, which repents after his preaching. Whether the statement in Malachi, "Have we not all one father?" was meant to include all men is debatable, but many accept it as such (Malachi 2:10). John 3:16 proclaims God's love for the world (*kosmos*). Paul's moving out from the Jewish community to the Gentile world was the practical working out of the universal nature of God's call. In Romans 1:19-20 and 2:12-16, he affirms that knowledge of God and the inner law are the possession of all men.

Thus we see that the idea of election cannot be understood apart from its connection with responsibility. Both Israel and the church bear a special responsibility for fulfilling the will of God. Second, the chosenness of one group cannot be understood apart from the larger background of God's concern for all men. It is not just Israel or the church that God loves, but the world. The special call to the church today is to make known in deed as well as word God's reconciling love to the entire world.

## "HOLY HISTORY" AND GENERAL HISTORY

Although we have in this chapter considered the idea of covenant more fully than that of history, the reason is that biblical history is intimately bound up with the idea of a special relation between God and man. The history of Israel as well as of the church is intimately related to God's call to man and man's response to God.

But what does "holy history" have to do with general history? We noted at the beginning of the chapter several attempts to relate biblical history and general history. The traditional way, of course, is to assume the historical accuracy of the biblical record and to judge other history by that history.

Another way of dealing with the two is to separate them and deal with them as different realities. Public history is then subject to the investigation by historians; holy history is not. Still another conclusion has been that the existential dimensions of faith—that is, those that affect me now—are all that matter and that historical matters are of no consequence for faith.

None of these attempts seems to me to provide an adequate approach to the problem we face. Increasingly theologians are saying that history as such—both biblical history and general history—must be taken seriously. Thus, the historian *as historian* must use his historical methodology and tools in dealing with biblical history. Instrumentally, the historian's skills are absolutely essential in determining context and background for particular events, ideas, and writings in the biblical record: thus historical knowledge actually contributes to faith. The historian's action at this point, however, is still as historian, not as believer. He must be free to work as a historian and not be forced to deny the authenticity and integrity of his calling as historian in order to bolster up the shaky historical foundations of faith.

There is another dimension to biblical thought, however, at which point the work of the historian ends and that of the believer (or theologian) begins. This has to do with the perspective from which the Bible views life and history. This faith perspective, if taken seriously, will color the believer's view of all life and history. The perspective that comes from "holy history" thus becomes the one from which all history is understood.

We will have much more to say in the following chapter about the Christian perspective on general history. We have already noted in this one that the concept of holy history— the call to and response of a special people—does not necessarily deny the relationship of God to all people and all history. The prophets often said quite the contrary. The participation by Israel, and later by the church, in the covenant relationship, rather, placed upon them special responsibility.

## CONCLUSION

We may conclude, I believe, that the designation "holy history," though one commonly used in recent years, must be qualified or at least properly understood to be acceptable for our time. The life and history of Israel and the church are holy in the sense in which the word is sometimes used— namely, "set apart." This set-apartness, however, is for the purpose of affirming what God has done and what he wishes to do for all mankind. Indeed, as we shall see in the next chapter, it may involve in a special way the *identification* of what God is in fact doing in the world today. The special gift of the man of faith is partly his ability to see and hear. This, at least, is what many theologians are saying today, and to an interpretation of their point of view we now turn.

# Chapter V

# GOD AND SECULAR HISTORY

As we examined the concept of "holy history" in Chapter IV, it became increasingly evident that many questions must be raised concerning the adequacy of the idea. So persistent have these questions become to many theologians that they have ceased to use the term altogether. Those who have gone furthest in their reaction to the perspective emphasized by a previous generation of theologians are sometimes called "theologians of secularity."

What is the basic point of view of those who represent this trend in theological thought? William Fennell, a Canadian theologian, summarizes the understanding of God's relation to the world increasingly held by theologians today. "If in

Jesus Christ the *world* has been reconciled to God," he writes, "there are no longer two realms, a godly and an ungodly, standing in irreconcilable enmity toward one another." Rather, he continues, there is only one realm of life—"the created, creaturely, fallen," but a realm also "reconciled and renewed," over which "Jesus Christ reigns as Savior and Lord." [1]

We may identify three major degrees of response to this current emphasis on secularization in relation to Christian faith. Some theologians, while unable to ignore the increasing secularization of life, nevertheless wistfully hope that we can somehow return to the days when traditional churchly language was part and parcel of daily existence. Others agree that all life is God's and that there really should be no radical break between the sacred and the secular, but they are reluctant to glorify the secular, believing that all life needs transformation. They hesitate in giving up traditional *meanings,* though they recognize the necessity of expressing these meanings in modern terminology. Finally, there is a third group who would set no limits to the secular understanding of life and would express the Christian gospel completely in secular or this-worldly terms.[2]

However one responds to the process of secularization, whether he be theologian or ordinary churchman, he cannot ignore it. Our time is one in which existence is seen primarily in "this worldly" terms. Often those who attempt to hold to an "other worldly" view of life find themselves living in two realms, the secular and the religious, with the two seldom, except on Sunday, being interrelated. God *is* dead for many people in terms of their actual living, regardless of how tenaciously they hold onto their expressed belief that he, after all, is alive.

It is important, therefore, that Christians come to grips with the process of secularization and relate Christian faith to the secular world. No understanding of history that fails to

---

[1] From "The Theology of True Secularity," by William O. Fennell, in *New Theology No. 2,* eds. Martin E. Marty and Dean G. Peerman (New York: The Macmillan Company, 1965), p. 36. Italics mine.

[2] See *The Secularization of History: An Introduction to the Theology of Friedrich Gogarten,* by Larry Shiner (Nashville: Abingdon Press, 1966), p. 175.

take this task seriously is relevant for our day. God must be seen in relation to all of existence, or he ceases to be relevant at all.

## BIBLICAL ROOTS OF SECULARIZATION

At the simplest level, the relation of God to all life and history can be seen in what in Chapter IV we spoke of as the universalism of the Bible, expressed in the assertion that Abraham was to be the medium of God's blessing to all the families of the earth (Genesis 12:3). Amos' view of God's concern is enlarged to include the surrounding nations (Amos 1:3 through 2:3), as was that of the pre-Exilic Isaiah (Isaiah 13 through 21) and of Jeremiah (Jeremiah 46 through 51). Cyrus the Persian was to the post-Exilic Isaiah God's anointed (Isaiah 45:1). Israel was to be "a light to the nations" (Isaiah 42:6). Jonah was sent to the "heathen" city of Nineveh, and so on.

God's universal concern for man would not necessarily, however, lead to the position held by the secular theologians, who go further in their analysis of the Hebrew-Christian tradition. Hebrew thought, they say, is not really a religion in the sense that most religions seek to control God and nature. Rather, Hebrew thought emphasizes God's approach to man so as to liberate him to be as God intended him to be, free in relation to both God and his fellow men.[3] The process of freeing the Jew, seen especially in prophetic religion, and later the Christian, from ecclesiatical control is, these theologians conclude, the secularization which has gone on during the entire Hebrew-Christian history, but especially during the last century.

The distinctions made by Harvey Cox, popularizer of the theology of secularization in the United States, between *secularism* and *secularization,* are generally accepted by exponents of the secular understanding of life. Both terms refer to "this age" or "the time of this world," but the two are not the same. *Secularization* means the freeing of society from its dependence

[3] See *Faith in a Secular Age,* by Colin Williams (New York: Harper Chapel Books, 1966), pp. 47 ff.

on a superstitious belief in the controlling influence of super-natural powers. Through secularization, man is freed to be his true self, a responsible being. *Secularism,* on the other hand, indicates any new nontheistic religion whose adherents seek to impose their views on others. The denial of religion in communist countries, for example, becomes a new religion. Secularism is the making of anything transient into something worshiped as permanent.[4]

Cox argues that one step in the process of secularization is to be found in the Hebrew view of creation, which is unlike the ideas in creation stories of other Near Eastern religions. Creation is God's handiwork, according to Genesis, but God is not identified with it; rather, man is put in charge of it. This interpretation, Cox argues, is a secular interpretation of creation. Or to place it in the context of an earlier chapter, life is viewed in terms of history, not nature. Creation is seen as a part of the vast sweep of God's dealing with the world, not as some manifestation of or emanation from the gods.

A further step in secularization is found in the Exodus, which Cox interprets as the "desacralization of politics." God was the only king; no one ruled by "divine right," only by the power derived from Yahweh. A third step Cox believes took place in the covenant with Moses, when God was so ab-solutized that all of man's values were thereby relativized (even his "religious values"). Man could no longer depend on the gods whom images made concrete. He must depend on God alone, who is made known through the Law. Cox fails to take into account that there was a tendency to absolutize the Law itself, especially in later Judaism, though he would insist rightly that this was not the original intent of the Covenant.

What Cox and others are saying is that the Hebrew faith was not a religion in the common use of the word, though it developed into a religion and was sometimes almost overcome by religious institutionalism. Originally it was a total view

---

[4] See *The Secular City,* by Harvey Cox (New York: The Macmillan Company, 1966), pp. 20-21 and *passim.* See also *The New Creation as Metropolis,* by Gibson Winter (New York: The Macmillan Company, 1963), pp. 34-64.

of life, with the sacred and the secular blended together. All created things were sacred because they were God's; yet all created things were secular because they were to be used by man. There was one history—a history at the same time sacred (in that it was centered in the activity of God) and secular (in that it was not, like Greek and Roman mythology, concerned just with the life of the gods but rather with the relation of God to man).

A brief look at some of the major events of Hebrew history, a history usually called "holy," soon shows those events to be related to the everyday life of the people, not to organized or institutional religion: God's call to Abraham to go to a new country and Abraham's obedience; Moses' response to God's call to lead the Israelites out of slavery; the generosity of an alien, Cyrus the Persian, in making possible the Second Exodus after the Babylonian captivity; the political zeal of the Maccabees which temporarily freed the nation from Greek rule (recorded in the Apocrypha). Jesus did not operate as part of the religious establishment—neither that of the priests nor of the official sects such as the Pharisees—but as carpenter turned teacher. The entire history we now call *holy* was as *secular* as it could be.

Religious institutions began to take shape early in the history of Israel, with a break between the priestly and prophetic strains of thought. This conflict can be seen especially in Amos (eighth century). From the time of Ezra and Nehemiah in the fifth century B.C., the priestly-nationalistic-legalistic coalition predominated, though such books as Ruth and Jonah indicate that prophetic thought was not gone.

Jesus joined the prophetic tradition by rejecting the absolutizing of the Law and the religious institution. The best known statement illustrating this point is "The sabbath was made for man, not man for the sabbath. . . ." (Mark 2:27). Paul continued the process of freeing man from bondage to such exterior norms as the Law by insisting that now man could be responsible under God, not the Law:

> During our minority we were slaves to the elemental
> spirits of the universe, but when the term was com-

69

> pleted, God sent his own Son, born of a woman, born
> under the law, to purchase freedom for the subjects
> of the law, in order that we might attain the status of
> sons. (Galatians 4:3-5; *The New English Bible*)

Let us carry Paul's analogy a bit further. A man in an ecclesiastically controlled culture is like a dependent child: he is given minimum freedom to make his own decisions, and his life is, by and large, controlled by the priests and their cultic practices, designed to propitiate the gods. When a child becomes a true son—that is, achieves the status of independence—he is free to live a responsible life. He may become irresponsible, to be sure; but unless he has that option, he cannot exercise responsibility.

So with the Christian man: he is freed from the law (which Paul saw as binding and arbitrary) to be a true son of God. He is given a new status before God in Jesus Christ, just as the son who has achieved his majority is given a new status before his earthly father. Both the child and the free man can now take responsibility for themselves, and must do so.

Secularization, according to these writers, therefore, is the process by which the gospel frees men to live by faith. The man of faith is freed from the domination of religion (cult, law, institution) in order that he may live in relation to God and his fellow men as a free man.

## CONTEMPORARY EXPONENTS OF SECULARITY

Let us now review briefly the ideas of some of the exponents of secularization, which came into prominence in the 1950's following an over-emphasis on holy history.

The upsurge of the emphasis may be found during World War II, though the first expression of criticism against religion as opposed to faith is found earlier in the writings of Karl Barth. Friedrich Gogarten and Dietrich Bonhoeffer, in his later writings, are generally considered the seminal thinkers in regard to secularization. Gogarten and Bonhoeffer worked independently on the same themes, and came to similar conclusions, namely (as Larry Shiner has aptly put it), "that the ideal of autonomy and freedom is not in itself the enemy of

Christian faith but an approximation of the worldliness and responsibility of faith itself." [5]

As early as 1942, Bonhoeffer wrote to his student Eberhard Bethge concerning his growing resistance to "religiosity." Later in prison, he returned to the theme—especially in the letters —with enough clarity that this phase of his thought has been seized upon with greater enthusiasm than perhaps any other. Bonhoeffer was concerned that the basic meaning of faith be free from its identification with religiosity (or piosity) so that it could truly confront the world.

As Colin Williams has pointed out, Bonhoeffer remained aware of the dangers of an easy alliance of Christian faith with the world. He was far too conscious of the capitulation of the German church under Hitler. Ironically, however, he also knew that the attempt to keep the church out of the world and in its own peculiar religious realm "had resulted in its acquiescence in the false worldly values of Hitlerism."

Bonhoeffer therefore looked for a new way of structuring the relationship of church and world—"in the sense that it would cut through this sacred-secular dichotomy and would dispense with outward religiosity in order to free itself for the real world of human existence—the secular world." [6]

Working both independently and under the influence especially of Bonhoeffer, other thinkers have advanced similar theses—for example, Cornelius van Peursen and Arend Th. van Leeuwen in The Netherlands, Gerhard Ebeling in Germany, and Harvey Cox in the United States. More recently and more radically Paul van Buren, William Hamilton, and Thomas Altizer have presented ideas that have led to the journalistic "death of God" theology.

There are, of course, many variations among the exponents of a secular interpretation of Christianity. It is generally agreed, however, that the domination of life and history by organized religion is ending, and that end is interpreted as good. The immediate forms of religion were always in danger

[5] From *The Secularization of History: An Introduction to the Theology of Friedrich Gogarten,* by Larry Shiner, p. 217.
[6] *Faith in a Secular Age,* by Colin Williams, p. 57.

of being substituted for faith in God alone, and it may be that we are now being freed for true faith. Further, the biblical faith is seen not simply as operating in the past but as continuing into the present.

But the most important—and perhaps the least controversial —emphasis of the new theologians is that the division of sacred and secular is destroyed and God's lordship over all history is asserted. As Gayraud Wilmore puts it, the true secularity of the church lies "in believing and acting out realistically the message that Jesus Christ is not only the Lord of the church but is also the Lord of General Motors and the Democratic Party and is working quite outside the church as such, to fulfill the reconciliation of the world." [7]

## EXCESSES AND DANGERS

One of the great gifts of the secular theologians is to free many sincere Christians to enjoy the world, for much that went under the name of other-worldly pietism was opposed to any such enjoyment. Yet it must be remembered in an appraisal of both the past and the present that there are some things about this world which the Christian cannot accept. The Christian in a communist country, for example, faces the problem of having to live in a world which sets up a rival faith. But the Christian in the noncommunist country faces a similar problem as he both affirms the goodness of life in his nation and at the same time questions the injustices and the temptation to idolatry nationalism inevitably creates. There is a danger that both the theologian and the ordinary Christian will not only *accept* but *approve* all of the world in which he lives. Harvey Cox has been accused of romanticizing the secular city in something of the way a past generation romanticized nature. Neither nature nor the secular city is unqualifiedly good, and the Christian must oppose the slums, the ghettos, the injustices in employment, the corruption in city hall, and a hundred other wrongs which any modern city contains.

[7] From *The Secular Relevance of the Church*, by Gayraud S. Wilmore (Philadelphia: The Westminster Press, 1962), p. 21.

Excesses occur on yet another level—namely, that of denying uniqueness to the Christian message. In its most radical aspect, this denial leads to the death of God proclamation. Others do not go so far but do fail to recognize that there *is* a unique Christian interpretation of life and history and that to refuse to come to grips with it is to step outside the Christian perspective.

While recognizing the excesses of the secular theologians, we must also be aware of the dangers of not accepting this broader understanding of God's relationship to history. We have noted in the previous chapter some of these dangers, not the least of which are the pride and self-satisfaction that come from being in the "in crowd"—God's chosen group.

An even more subtle danger is that the institutions of the religious movement will be idolized, that what is instrumental will be identified with the absolute. It was at least in part this fear of absolutizing the temporary which led Bonhoeffer to propose a nonreligious Christianity. Karl Barth is likewise strong in his opposition to religion, which he interprets as man's efforts to reach God as opposed to Christianity's emphasis on accepting God's grace.

One can go to excesses at this point, also, for it is questionable whether any of the enterprises in which man participates can avoid being institutionalized. Nevertheless, the caution which Barth, Bonhoeffer, and many others provide in relation to the institutions of religion is a word well spoken.

## GOD AND THE WORLD

The position of the secular theologians, on the side of God's universal action in history, is not unlike that of Paul in Romans 1:19-20, as translated in *The New English Bible:* "For all that may be known of God by men lies plain before their eyes; indeed God himself has disclosed it to them. His invisible attributes, that is to say his everlasting power and deity, have been visible, ever since the world began, to the eye of reason, in the things he has made."

That is, God is accessible to man in the very created order of life itself. Not everyone acknowledges his presence, to be sure, but this in no way negates the reality of God. Indeed, we may go a step beyond Paul and affirm that there is a real sense in which God works through all men whether they recognize it or not. If we really believe that God is responsible for all things—that he is the "ground of being"—then to affirm otherwise is to contradict our basic premise concerning God as creator and sustainer of life.

Let us illustrate in the field of the arts. Arthur Miller's *Death of a Salesman* has been used often as an aid to understanding life from a Christian perspective, though it is clear that Miller did not intend the play to do so. One of the recurring themes of the play is the failure of Willy Loman, a salesman, and his family to see themselves honestly. To use traditional Christian language, there is no repentance here except in the case of Biff, one of the sons. He finally sees himself for what he is, and the process of new life then begins.

Willy Loman never really faces up to who he is, however, and commits suicide. One may well speculate that this may be the only honest act of Willy's life, for through it he frees his wife, Linda, to be the person she could never have been while he lived. Perhaps there is a kind of resurrection in the play not only in the case of Biff but also in the case of Linda.

Of course, we take to an art form much from our own background and perception, but so do we in all of life. The important thing is that God can and does speak to us through the work of an artist—believer or nonbeliever; that is, he speaks through the secular.

Just so, the persons participating in some event of history may not have the slightest understanding that what is happening is a means for God's self-revelation. Certainly the Egyptians of the Exodus did not. Nor is it likely that Nero comprehended at all what was happening in first-century Rome. This lack of understanding does not mean, however, that God is not at work in the event.

It should be made clear that, when I speak of the "activity of God," I do not necessarily mean direct cause and effect. For example, a push may be what starts a rock rolling down a hill; but many other factors go into the action: gravity, the existence of a slope, a relatively unobstructed course, the shape of the stone, and so on. If we are not careful, we will fail to see God at work in any action unless we can identify him as the one who, figuratively, gives the push, even though the actual push is only one factor in the total operation.

The objective reality of God at work in history can probably not be demonstrated, certainly not to the satisfaction of the positivist or of the strict empiricist. The point here is that, as we have seen earlier, there are many perspectives from which one may view history; and the perspective of Hebrew-Christian faith is one of these. Once we have accepted the reality of God as the ground of all being, however, we are free to understand all life and history as a manifestation of the divine reality. Thus we perceive the activity of God where others may see only the random activity of chance. This does not mean that we will understand fully or that the mystery of life is removed. It means simply that we can begin to bring some meaning out of that which without God would hardly be anything other than meaningless.

## THE MEANING OF HISTORY

If we are right in concluding that there are not two histories but one—and I believe we are—and if we then move on to try to discern the activity of God in all of history, where do we begin in our interpretive efforts? Traditional Christian language speaks of God's action in such terms as *creation, judgment, redemption* and *reconciliation, sanctification* and *growth.* First, how is God's action seen in creation?

*Creation* is not just a past event but is a present reality. The creative process can be observed constantly in nature—in conception, prenatal growth, and birth; in the annual return of spring; in the exploding universe of stellar space where new stars are being born. Creativity can be seen in a derived sense through man's work: the splitting of the atom; the synthesizing of chemicals; the making of new strains of plants and animals; the possibility of producing life through artificial means; the production of a work of art. Though none of these phenomena *proves* the reality of God, through the eyes of faith we can see that reality.

75

We also see the action of God through *judgment.* There is not always—perhaps not usually—a direct cause and effect relationship between sin and judgment. The human temptation is to seize upon the defeat of our enemy (for example, Germany by the Allies in World War I and World War II) as a judgment of God, which it may be. (Germany's defeat *was* a judgment, as historian Butterfield points out, on Prussian militarism.) We must be very careful, however, always to be aware that all of us are under judgment.

> . . . if Germany is under judgment so are all of us—the whole of our existing order and the very fabric of our civilisation. If once we admit that the moral factor operates in this way in history at all, then we to-day must feel ourselves to be living in one of those remarkable periods when judgment stalks generally through the world. . . .[8]

The racial crisis as a judgment on two centuries of United States injustice toward the Negro; the unrest in Africa as a judgment against the evils of nineteenth-century colonialism; the large-scale defection of intellectuals from the church as a judgment against the church's failure to be intellectually responsible in a scientific age—these are only a few illustrations of judgment on both church and world.

If we see judgment, we can also see and experience *redemption, reconciliation,* and *new life,* or the continuing reality of the Resurrection. Though we expect, or at least hope, to see this renewal in the church, it is also happening in other contexts. The work of renewal is no less God's activity when the context is a secular group, for only God can bring about new life.

James V. Clark, a behavioral scientist who is chairman of a graduate program in business, reports the kinds of remarks made by people who have participated in sensitivity training groups, in which the emphasis is on interpersonal relationships. The following are representative: [9]

---

[8] From *Christianity and History,* by Herbert Butterfield, p. 52.
[9] From "Toward a Theory and Practice of Religious Experiencing," by James V. Clark, in *Challenges of Humanistic Psychology,* ed.

A CHINESE BANKER AND PHILOSOPHER, AGED
FORTY-FIVE:
I have studied philosophy all my life and now, right
now, I feel the hands of Christ are upon me. You—
your hands are the hands of Christ.

A MANAGEMENT CONSULTANT, AGED
THIRTY-FIVE:
I *saw* this old man today in our afternoon group. He is
a, a *jerk*. He is a fundamentalist, and he is *proud* of
it. And I, I (*crying*) *loved* him. I loved him. I love
him.

A LAWYER, AGED THIRTY-FOUR:
It's like I am on two ladders, like I *must* be on two
ladders. One is my family and the other is the men
I work with. And I am on these ladders and looking
up, and at the top, at the top (*cries*), is a big light
and it's "Eli!" (*Cries, smiles.*) You know, I was
brought up a good orthodox boy, and I never saw
God before. I never did.

God's action can also be seen in *growth*. Even the process of
physical growth declares that the universe is alive, not dead,
and testifies to the living Lord of a living universe. Growth
of persons into more adequate expressions of being also witnesses to the activity of God.

One of the remarkable stories of the modern world is that
of Helen Keller. It is also the story of Anne Sullivan, whose
patience and persistence led to the unlocking of the life of the
child Helen. Is this a "religious" story or a "secular" story?
The question is irrelevant, for the significant thing is that
amazing growth occurred in the life of a deaf and blind girl.

## CONCLUSION

"You know how to interpret the appearance of the sky,
but you cannot interpret the signs of the times" (Matthew

James Bugental (New York: McGraw-Hill Book Company, Copyright ©
1967), pp. 253-254. Used by permission of McGraw-Hill Book Company.

16:3*b*). These words are attributed to Jesus in conversation with representatives of the religious establishment of his day. The kingdom of God was breaking into history—but they could not see what was happening!

It is never easy for organized religion to recognize its function of pointing to the reality and activity of God in the world. To do so may seem to diminish the importance of the institution, and perhaps it does. Nevertheless, to help persons "discern the time," that is, to see what is happening in their midst today, is the work to which the church is called. As Gibson Winter puts it, "The work of the servant church is to engage the world in reflection on the meaning of its history, to summon men to the search for the meaning of the events in which they are engaged." [10]

---

[10] From *The New Creation as Metropolis,* by Gibson Winter, p. 71.

# Chapter VI

# PROBLEMS IN HISTORICAL UNDERSTANDING

One of the obvious concepts emerging from our consideration of the meaning of history is that all of us are *personally
involved in history,* or, more appropriately, in histories. A
second key concept is that we inevitably *view history from
some perspective.* This perspective influences our reading,
study, teaching, and recording of history. Even if we have
no particular stake in an event such as an accident, for instance, we cannot report all details, because we did not see
everything; therefore our report is incomplete and biased.

Another dimension to this concept is that we also view
history from a perspective that has meaning to us. We have
our own inner history—that in which we are personally involved; and it is difficult if not impossible to escape it
completely.

A third key concept deals with the *pattern of history*. We have noted that the mode of interpreting history character-istic of the Hebrew-Christian tradition is linear, not cyclical. That is, history is seen as "going somewhere."

A fourth motif is *meaning in history*. We have repeatedly maintained that in the Christian view of history meaning is found as the course of human events is seen in relation to God.

A fifth motif has to do with *the relationship of "holy" history and general history*. I have maintained not only that biblical, or holy, history provides a perspective from which to view all of history, but that all of history must be under-stood as the arena of God's activity.

In this chapter, we shall consider four separate but related problems of historical understanding: (1) revelation and his-tory; (2) the meaning of life and history in relation to sin and evil; (3) the sovereignty of God and history; (4) the kingdom of God and the end of history. The basic meaning of each problem must be considered briefly as well as its relevance for a Christian view of history.

## REVELATION AND HISTORY

The Christian understanding of revelation centers in God's disclosure of himself to man. Revelation cannot be under-stood apart from its relation to history; nor can history from a Christian point of view be understood apart from the cen-trality of revelation. Revelation is not just a past event, how-ever. The Fourth Gospel speaks of the Christ so that those who believe now "may have life in his name" (John 20:31*b*).

*The Nature of Revelation.* The Bible is not a book of meta-physics; it is not concerned with proving the existence of God nor with philosophically deducing his attributes. It does not discuss abstract ideas, but tells how God has acted in his dealing with man. The experience of revelation—that is, a perception of and response to the living God—is the reality to which both Old and New Testaments witness.

The trend in Jewish thought just prior to the Christian era was to codify the way in which man must respond to

God. This growing legalism tended to make of Torah—the living word of God—a set of rules and regulations. We can see a similar move in the New Testament, from the *experience* of faith to *statements about* faith. Throughout most of the New Testament, the word *faith* is an active and personal word, concerned with trust, commitment, relationship. That is, faith is a personal encounter with and response to what God has done and is now doing.

By the time of the book of Jude, however, the meaning of faith had begun to change. In this early second-century book, faith has become "the faith which was once for all delivered to the saints" (Jude 1:3). Now faith is something to defend, not just to experience. Revelation in the second-century church was near to being equated with the record of revelation, or *propositions about God*. The *personal* was being replaced by the *propositional*.

The two views of revelation, personal and propositional, are common in the church today. Some of the Reformers, especially Luther, tired to break the propositional view; but in the century following the Reformation, the importance of the written word became only more rigidly held. As liberal theology of the late nineteenth and early twentieth centuries accepted the historical criticism of the Bible, fundamentalism, an even more rigid literalism, arose. One of the tasks of recent theology, therefore, has been to redefine the nature of revelation. It has done this by a return to the essentially biblical idea that the content of revelation does not consist of propositions about God but rather of an experience of the living God himself, especially in the Incarnation in Jesus Christ.

To distinguish between the two views of revelation, let us consider the ordinary ways by which we come to know another person. A first level of knowledge may be when we read about him, perhaps in the newspaper. Or someone who has met the other person may report to us what he knows about the third person. In neither of these ways do we come to know the person himself—only what other people say about him.

When we meet the person himself, we may discover that what we have read or heard about him is helpful in our relationship with him. On the other hand, we may find that our previous perception of him was faulty and we return to written records about him with a different perspective. In no case is someone else's report an adequate substitute for personal knowledge.

Revelation, then, is both a recorded event of the past and an event in our lives. Unless, however, it becomes for us a continuing experience, we are living on capital borrowed from the past.

*Report and Encounter.* This nonpropositional approach to revelation does not mean that language has no relationship to God's self-disclosure. The perception of meaning leads to a proposition even if one never utters it, as, when seeing a rose, a person responds, however unconsciously, "beautiful rose!"

The report of the reality of revelation is a part of the experience, for God may enter into the report as well as into the original experience. The biblical records, therefore, may (1) help produce in us an experience similar to the one to which the written record points; (2) prepare us for identifying our own experiences; (3) help us verify the genuineness of our own experience of the reality of God.

To illustrate: One of the buildings I had looked forward to seeing perhaps more than any other on my first visit to Europe was the Colosseum in Rome. The pictures I had seen and the reports I had read prompted me to seek out the real thing. They also prepared me for identifying my experience. Had I never seen the pictures or read about it, I might well have said, had I stumbled across it by accident, "What's that?" But I *knew* it the moment I saw it, for it looked precisely like the pictures in my early history books. My past response to reports about the building helped me identify my own experience as genuine.

Thus we see that both the historical and the contemporary aspects of the meaning of revelation are important. An emphasis on revelation as personal reminds us that nothing substitutes for our inner response. The historical dimension of revelation provides for us the clue for understanding our response.

The event from the past that provides the clue to a Christian understanding of history is the life, death, and resurrection of Jesus Christ. We enter into that experience partly by reading the report of the Bible and partly by our own personal response to God. Our response is personal but not private: that is, it must be tested both by our contemporaries and by what we learn from history. It is important, therefore, that we depend neither on our own subjective experience nor on the report of what happened in the past, but on both. In so doing, we are related to the past and at the same time we receive guidance for viewing the present.

*General or Special?* Another question of significance for our study has to do with what traditionally has been known as "general" and "special" revelation. The usual way of explaining the difference in the two is that general revelation refers to that knowledge of God available to all mankind through the power of reason, while special revelation is that which centers in Jesus as the Christ.

Although this distinction is not held with any rigidity by most Protestant theologians today, it does provide a convenient way of indicating the relation of revelation to history. It may be, however, that the word *general* is not the best one to indicate the knowledge of God available to all men. *General* may mean only a vague abstraction as opposed to *specific* or *unique* or *particular*. A word that seems to express more adequately the idea of revelation in all of life and history is *universal.* Paul Tillich uses this term to mean all of God's self-disclosure that prepares for the revelation in Jesus Christ. That revelation for the Christian gives meaning to all others, but it is not the only way in which God is known.[1]

Schubert Ogden, contemporary American theologian, puts this relationship between universal revelation and that in Jesus Christ in a meaningful way for the modern Christian concerned for the relevance of faith to contemporary existence: ". . . the church stands by the claim that the decisive manifestation of this divine word is none other than the human word

[1] See *Systematic Theology,* by Paul Tillich (Chicago: The University of Chicago Press, 1951) , Vol. I, pp. 138-39.

of Jesus of Nazareth and thence of its own authentic proclamation. But the point of this claim is not that the Christ is manifest only in Jesus and nowhere else, but that the word addressed to men *everywhere* in all the events of their lives, is none other than the word spoken in Jesus and in the preaching and sacraments of the church." [2]

Thus we are alerted not only to the importance of revelation *in* all of history as well as in nature; we need also to take account of revelation for all history. That is, the activity of God can be seen in all of life and history, but one interpretation of that activity is found in the revelation unique to Christian faith. On the other hand, all of life and history are made intelligible for the Christian as he looks at them from the Christian perspective. Christian revelation is related to history because it is in history that Jesus Christ lived out his life. It is related to history further because it is from that event that all of history derives its meaning for the Christian.

This is not meant to imply that God uses only the traditional symbols of the Christian community as bearers of his revelation today. Rather, as Tillich writes, "There is no reality, thing, or event which cannot become a bearer of the mystery of being and enter into a revelatory correlation." [3]

The traditional symbols in terms of words, visual symbols, or meanings are the means by which the Christian interprets the meaning of life and history, however. The church, as we saw in the previous chapter, bears the responsibility of helping discern what God is doing in our time as well as in the past. As it carries out this task, it will inevitably do so in the light of the revelation which called it into being—that is, Jesus Christ.

## EVIL AND SIN

One might say that, whereas the purpose of revelation is the *illumination* of history, evil and sin, with their consequent suffering, *obscure* history's meaning. The nature of what is

---

[2] From *Christ Without Myth*, by Schubert M. Ogden (New York: Harper & Row, 1961), p. 156.

[3] From *Systematic Theology*, by Paul Tillich, Vol. I, p. 118.

revealed can help bring meaning out of the chaos that widespread evil and suffering seem to imply.

*Evil* is a broader term than *sin*, since it denotes all that thwarts God's will for man's good. There is, so far as I can determine, no objective way of defining evil; the simplest definition of the term is that which causes man to suffer. Sin, on the other hand, is that which breaks man's relationship with God and with other men. Sins are acts that grow out of man's sinful state.

The usual way of explaining sin is to attribute it to the freedom God has given man either to accept or to reject his creatureliness and his dependence on God. While this explanation of sin is not complete, it is at least logical. There is, however, no logical way to explain the existence of evil, for logic implies a sufficient cause; and it is difficult if not impossible for man to understand why the world is not set up for his complete benefit.

Although the existence of freedom offers part of the solution to the reality of sin, it does not offer a readily acceptable answer to natural evil; though there are those who would extend the reality of freedom to all reality. In this panpsychic interpretation of reality, all existents—rocks, ants, chimpanzees, men—possess the freedom to act in harmony with all other reality, or to rebel against it.

Nor is there a simple explanation for man's persistence in harming himself and his neighbor. Why does man still insist on settling his disputes through war? Why is the white majority so blind to injustices against the Afro-American? Above all towers the modern mushroom cloud as a symbol of the power man now has to destroy himself and all his works.

The common solution to the problem of evil (which was really no solution) until comparatively recently was to blame it on evil spirits and demons—"principalities," "powers," "world rulers of this present darkness," "the spiritual hosts of wickedness in the heavenly places" (Ephesians 6:12). This belief entered Hebrew thought as Israel came into contact with the dualistic religions of the East, especially Zoroastrianism. Such religions contained vivid pictures of the warfare of the good and evil spirits, Zoroaster even teaching that there were two primary gods, the Good and the Evil, with the Good ultimately to triumph.

The problem of evil is, of course, related to what one believes about God and God's relationship to both the natural order and the life of man (history) : either God is able to prevent evil and will not, or else he is willing and cannot. If the former is the case, he is not all merciful; if the latter, he is not all powerful. This dilemma suggests the need for a new way of thinking about God. Four solutions, all oversimplified in their statement here, may be noted. (1) As suggested above, evil is due to the rebellion of certain creatures against God, creatures who later bring evil upon man. The elaboration of this thesis by John Milton in "Paradise Lost" has perhaps had more influence on the persistence of this theory than has the Bible itself, which does not elaborate the view though much of it takes it for granted. (2) Evil is a necessary part of any finite order: you simply cannot have perfection in a *created* order, for perfection belongs only to God. (3) Evil is thought of only as an illusion and will be so recognized when men see from the viewpoint of eternity. (4) There is no theoretical answer to evil, which can be interpreted only as a mystery to bring men to obedience to and trust in God.[4]

There are difficulties with all of these solutions, especially with the first, third, and fourth. We have already seen how the first simply pushes the problem back to the question why certain spirits are allowed to afflict man. The third, that evil will be considered only an illusion from the standpoint of eternity, is not really an answer for it does not solve the problem of the present reality of the illusion. Nor is it really a solution to say that evil is a mystery that cannot be explained.

This leaves us with the answer that evil is a necessary part of any finite, or created, order. Although this is no ultimate answer, it seems to be the best available. God could not create a perfect order, else he would be duplicating himself. Since the created order, according to the Hebrew-Christian interpretation, is not an extension of God, but is his creation, it is of necessity less than God.

[4] See *A Handbook of Theological Terms,* by Van A. Harvey (New York: The Macmillan Company, 1966) , p. 237.

Twentieth-century philosopher Charles Hartshorne has developed an understanding of omnipotence or God's power different from conventional answers. Hartshorne believes that the idea of God as unchanging is unfortunate, since God would thus be a static reality, rather than dynamic, living, and responsive to man. God, Hartshorne believes, accepted the limitation of imperfection in the created order by the act of creation itself, since that order would be less than God. Because of who he is and because of the nature of the created order, God cannot prevent suffering. God therefore suffers with man, for the "tragedies of existence are themselves known and felt as tragedies within the divine life." The key to understanding the character of God, then, is "divine suffering." [5]

An analogy in human relationships may be helpful at this point. If man were not capable of entering into relationships of love and concern, he would probably never suffer as a result of the loss of another person. The more deeply one enters into such relationships, the more vulnerable one is to suffering. Even if there were no loss other than death—which is an inevitable part of human life—man would still be subject to suffering. God could, let us assume, have made man without feeling; but man would then have been something other than the man whom we know. If man were to have feelings at all—joy, creativity, satisfaction—then he must also experience suffering and tragedy. Being created in the image of God means the ability to share in both divine creativity and divine suffering.

What does this discussion of sin, evil, and suffering have to do with history? Simply this: being so much a part of history, they must be acknowledged even if there is no final solution to problems they raise. A Christian view of history does not provide an answer to evil, but it does change the question so that it is possible to deal with it. The problem of evil is closely related to the question of the sovereignty of God and thus with God's providential will, the question to which we now turn.

[5] See *ibid.*

## THE SOVEREIGNTY OF GOD

The term "sovereignty" is chosen over "omnipotence" for this section, and for good reason: one may be sovereign without controlling, while omnipotence generally includes control or at least the ability to control. For example, no sovereign ruler of a nation, even though he be a dictator, can control every action of his subjects unless they are under some form of thought control.

Roger Shinn, of Union Seminary in New York, has rightly observed, I believe, that the most important question in a Christian understanding of history is the sovereignty of God. "If God rules the world," Shinn writes, "then provisional chaos and meaninglessness finally contribute to His purpose, and history is not in vain. If God does not rule, then whatever achievements may be wrought, the final words pronounced upon history are doom and despair." [6]

Shinn is also right, I believe, when he indicates that, first, because of the prevalence of evil, the sovereignty of God is not obvious in history. Too, the many aspects of history that seem to result from pure chance create real difficulties in regard to a doctrine of providence, which is closely related to God's sovereignty. Shinn observes, for example, that history seems to be subject both to "the impersonal processes of nature and to the capricious, inexplicable purposes of particular human beings." [7]

To be sure, some persons find no such "impersonal processes" or "capricious, inexplicable" human purposes. Rather, they see God's direct intervention in all events. If life is preserved by the presence of a sea gull on a lifeboat, it is God's intervention. If one soldier is killed and another spared in the same situation, God "took" one and "left" the other.

One holding such a view, however, must be prepared to give some reason why one person is singled out for favor and another is not. To reply that the individual affected by the event is not important, but that the event happens for the

[6] From *Christianity and the Problem of History*, by Roger L. Shinn, p. 247.
[7] *Ibid.*, p. 248.

glory of God is to ascribe capriciousness to God. Jesus was opposed to such a view: "for he makes his sun rise on the evil and on the good, and sends rain on the just and on the unjust," is the witness of Matthew 5:45b. Nor were those on whom the tower in Siloam fell worse than all those who dwelt in Jerusalem, according to Luke 13:4.

The reasons for some evil are obvious. For example, if a person lives near a known fault line in the earth's crust, he can anticipate the possibility of earthquake. If he lives on the seacoast where hurricanes have occurred in the past, he can expect similar occurrences. Careless driving causes accidents.

Although much evil can be explained, much cannot. We must not count on, or even attempt, an explanation of all events if we are to understand the sovereignty of God; rather, we must turn to God himself. I mean that we face life with certain presuppositions about the nature of God.

The first statement that must be made concerning the sovereignty of God is that he is sovereign love, that he relates to man in absolute love, and that this love is with man at all times. This is what Hartshorne means when he speaks of "divine suffering," for absolute love must involve suffering. The question one asks in a given situation of evil or suffering is, How is God as sovereign love at work in this situation to bring order out of chaos? Further, How can a situation that seems unqualifiedly bad be turned to good?

The second statement that may be made about God is that his will is not singular in the sense of having only one form of expression; rather, it is plural in its varieties of operation in human existence. Leslie Weatherhead, pastor of the City Temple in London for many years, differentiates three aspects of the will of God—the *intentional,* the *circumstantial,* and the *ultimate*—in lectures delivered to his congregation during World War II at the height of the bombing of London.

God's *intentional* will is that which he desires for man, but which is not completely implemented. The time to say, "Thou will be done," he writes, is not "when an airman is brought down in flames to meet an untimely death, but when the war is over and the young men of all nations can shake hands and begin together to build a new world. . . ." It is not when a baby dies "but when two young people take their little one before the altar to dedicate him or her to God. . . . Not when little children starve in Europe because of the circumstances of war . . . but when Europe is delivered at last from the ruthless heel of the oppressor. . . ." [8]

Regarding the *circumstantial* will of God, Weatherhead comments that the cross was the intention of evil men, not of God, but that under the circumstances Jesus could still pray "not as I will, but as thou wilt" (Matthew 26:39*b*). In other words, God's sovereignty is not necessarily to be sought in the *control* of the circumstances; for human freedom, chance, the finiteness of the created order, man's incomplete perspective —all may enter into the making of a particular situation. Rather, we see God's sovereign will done by the exercise of his love under the circumstances given.

Consider, for example, the matter of poverty. I do not believe that poverty is the will of God; nor do I believe that the people involved in "hard-core" poverty are usually able to extricate themselves from the hopeless situation of poverty. Yet there are ways by which the will of God can be done—provided other persons enter into the situation to provide new jobs, more creative relationships, better housing, tutoring for children, education in homemaking and finance. The trouble is that the affluent are not willing to pay the price to make it possible for God's will to be done under the kinds of circumstances that now exist in the ghettos of the cities and the forgotten hinterlands of rural areas.

Weatherhead points finally to God's *ultimate* will—that is, the carrying out of God's will in a way not now realized, perhaps in the actualization of God's kingdom. "Thy will *be* done," not "thy will *is* done," is the petition of the Lord's Prayer. His will can be seen, if only dimly, in the present ordering of life and history. It may be, as Reinhold Niebuhr and others have insisted, that God's perfect will is to be realized only beyond history.

These three meanings of God's will can be illustrated in the

[8] From *The Will of God*, by Leslie D. Weatherhead (Nashville: Abingdon Press, 1944), pp. 14-15 and *passim.*

life of a teen-age boy I know. I am sure God wanted John to be one of his choice creatures, for he was endowed with many of God's good gifts; but, because of tragic circumstances, these potentialities lie unrealized. When John was six, his father became permanently confined, because of an injury, to a hospital. When John was eleven, his mother deserted him and his three sisters, after living openly with a succession of men. John then lived in several foster homes, in one of which he was mistreated and from which he ran away.

By this time, John, a high-spirited and strong-willed boy, had been hurt so badly that there now followed a period of attempted rehabilitation—first in a preadoptive home from which he had to be removed and then in several foster homes, where, under the guidance of social agencies, John received the best of care. In spite of previous tragedy, God's purposes and will are being carried out in John's life as God's love reaches out to him from many sources.

I do not know how John figures in God's ultimate will, but I believe that he does. I believe that somehow what God intended will be brought to reality; how I do not know. But if human beings in their finiteness can feel so deeply for John, then God in his infinite mercy must be infinitely more concerned.

In speaking of God's ultimate will, we are brought face to face with another question that is crucial in our attempt to understand from a Christian perspective the meaning of history, namely, the idea of the kingdom of God. This is the traditional symbol pointing to the reality of God's reign, to his sovereignty over and beyond history as we know it.

## THE KINGDOM OF GOD

The Bible is concerned with the fulfillment of history, with how things will "come out in the end." This is known as eschatology, or the doctrine of the end of history, part of the linear view of history discussed in Chapter III. The Hebrew-Christian view is that history is moving toward something; it will have consummation some day.

The principal New Testament way of speaking about the eschaton (end of history) is in terms of the kingdom of God (or "kingdom of heaven," in Matthew). "Jesus came into Galilee proclaiming the Gospel of God: 'The time has come; the kingdom of God is upon you; repent, and believe the Gospel'" (Mark 1:14b-15; *The New English Bible*). The Greek word translated as *kingdom* in this and other passages is *basileia,* which literally means *sovereignty, royal power, dominion,* or *reigning.* It is not a static kingdom but, rather, the dynamic reigning of God.

The eschatological passages in the Synoptic Gospels seem to imply that the Kingdom would soon be completely fulfilled. (See Matthew 24, Mark 13, and Luke 21:1-36.) Paul's early letters, likewise, accept this view. (See especially 1 Thessalonians 4:13-18.) The Revelation to John is based on the assumption that all that is described is soon to happen (Revelation 22:20). Gradually, however, the expectation of the imminent end of the world lessened and eventually disappeared, only to recur periodically in Christian history, especially in times of change and trouble.

For the most part, however, some variation of Augustine's adaptation of New Testament eschatology has prevailed in the mainstream of Christianity. His idea of the earthly and the heavenly cities, with the two mingled together now, but with the heavenly one ultimately triumphant, provided a sound basis for a realistic view of this life and, at the same time, a clear sense of God's sovereignty. Augustine's view is not the only one held by biblical scholars and theologians today, however. Four main views, either current or from the immediate past, may be found in theological thought.

First, there are those who believe, like the British scholar C. H. Dodd, in a realized eschatology: "The Kingdom of God is not something yet to come," writes Dodd. "It came with Jesus Christ, and in its coming was perceived to be eternal in its quality. That eternal quality is manifested in time by the continuous life of the church, centered in the sacrament in which the crisis of the death and resurrection of Christ is perpetually made present." [9]

[9] From "The Kingdom of God and History," by C. H. Dodd, in *The Kingdom of God and History,* by H. G. Wood and others; No. 3,

One of the principal weaknesses of this view is the temptation to identify church and Kingdom. If the Kingdom was inaugurated with the preaching of Jesus, and if the church is the "Body of Christ" in any serious sense, then the Kingdom is likely to be seen in relationship to the church. Even if one distinguishes the institutional church from the church as Christ's Body, it is an easy step to the presumptuous conclusion that the institution itself is to be identified in some sense with the Kingdom.

The second view is generally called millennialism, after the thousand-year reign of God spoken of in Revelation 20. Millennialist interpreters of the Scriptures believe either that the "second coming" of Christ will precede this thousand years ("premillennialism") or that it will follow ("postmillennialism"). In either case, the millennium is supposed to follow a period in which conditions worsen and eventually become so bad that God intervenes.

Although a third position sees the Kingdom as primarily a future realization, there is an appreciation of the fact that the Kingdom has been inaugurated by the work of Jesus and consequently of the presence of the Kingdom, imperfect though it be, in life today. The primary emphasis, however, is on the future but gradual coming of the Kingdom, with the Kingdom closely identified with a utopian view of the ideal society. This concept of the Kingdom was closely related to the nineteenth-century idea of inevitable progress in society, and more often than not it was so conflated with man's accomplishments in the future that it became equated with the realization of man's hopes more than with the actualization of God's reign. This position was especially characteristic of liberal theology and the social gospel of the first three decades of the twentieth century, and has been revived by some of the secular theologians of our time.

One of liberalism's most effective critics, Reinhold Niebuhr, was quick to point out the virtue of this view, in spite of the general disrepute in which it is held today, namely, that both nature and the institutions of society may develop in time.

---

Oxford Conference Books (Chicago and New York: Willett, Clark & Company, 1938), p. 37.

Greek thought, with its cyclical view of time, had no such belief; and biblical thought saw the possibility of development only dimly. Modern culture, Niebuhr points out in *Faith and History*, is unique in its recognition that growth can and does take place. Niebuhr might have added that the idea of progress could hardly have developed outside a culture uninfluenced by the Hebrew view of history as moving somewhere.

In addition to its weak biblical basis, the fault in the idea of the gradual growth of the Kingdom is the illusion that growth is always good, that progress in such areas as technology frees life from its sin, and that man is self-fulfilling. The parable of the tares (Matthew 13:24-30) was ignored, though it contains a remarkable insight about life: Good and evil grow together, and it is not always as easy to distinguish the bad guys from the good guys as television westerns indicate.

The ambiguities of life may be seen by way of this illustration. An affluent society provides for young people the possibilities for life on a scale never before realized in society— increased physical growth, education, the enjoyment of the arts, opportunities for travel, and so on. On the other hand, all indications are that in no period of society has there been as much unrest and disaffection as in this generation of youth. The freedom modern culture affords can be both creative and destructive.

The fourth view of the kingdom of God seeks to avoid two extremes: (1) identifying the Kingdom with man's social progress and (2) the otherworldliness of millennialism. This fourth view retains the keen sense of involvement with historical activity characteristic of the liberal understanding of the Kingdom. It recognizes that the Kingdom is in one sense here, having been inaugurated by Jesus Christ. God is active in the world, and man can identify, respond to, and work with the direction of that activity. He can perform "signs of the Kingdom," and what he does is of genuine worth. Man, having been freed from the domination of ecclesiastical control, can now be a responsible son of God as he seeks to fulfill his destiny under God.

There is in the view, however, no illusion that man can create his own heaven on earth. An appreciation of man's accomplishments in history is retained, but the ultimate resolution of the ambiguities and contingencies of history is believed to be only a divine possibility. The consummation of history is in God's hands: God alone in the final analysis or in any ultimate sense fulfills history.

But will history be fulfilled from *within* or from *without?* That is, will the process of human events continue to the point at which God, through those events, brings his kingdom to reality? Or will there be a cessation of that stream of events and the introduction of another dimension (such as Augustine's heavenly city, for example) ?

The answer given to these questions is of considerably more significance to Christians who live on the brink of destruction than it is to those who are up against less obviously destructive forces. To the former, it appears unlikely that the process of human events is likely to be changed without radical discontinuity. For that matter, the individual Christian who faces death momentarily sees little fulfillment for himself within the process of time and history.

Many theologians, among them Paul Tillich and Reinhold Niebuhr, support the view that the fulfillment of history comes from outside the process of history. "By the symbol of the Resurrection," writes Niebuhr, "the Christian faith hopes for an eternity which transfigures, but does not annul, the temporal process." [10]

A final question concerning the kingdom of God remains: If the church and the Kingdom are not identified, what is their relationship? To answer this question, we return to the discussion in the two previous chapters of the relation of holy and secular history. The church has a peculiar responsibility for performing "signs of the Kingdom," but the Kingdom is not to be identified with the organized church. Just as John the Baptist, according to the Gospel of Matthew, announced the nearness of the Kingdom outside the religious structures of his day, so may the Kingdom break in from outside the organized religious structures of our day. Many articulate churchmen hold that the Kingdom is more likely to appear

[10] From *Faith and History*, p. 237.

today outside the church, which is in danger both of becoming so concerned with its own life that it loses its mission and of failing to apprehend how judgment is aimed both at history and at itself.

The church and those responsible for its life are under judgment if they do not faithfully proclaim the reality of the Kingdom and that to which it points, the sovereignty of God. This proclamation is partly through words—worship and preaching, instruction and nurture, evangelism and verbal witness.

The proclamation must also be through acts—through involvement in the struggles for equality by minority groups, for the alleviation of poverty, for the easing of international tensions. The real issues of life today are within the political and social structures; and if the church is not involved in dealing with these issues, it will prove itself increasingly irrelevant. It is on this level that the church is least likely to perform signs of the Kingdom.

The kingdom of God is not, as the social gospel interpreted it, just the realization of a better society; unless it is related to society in a realistic manner, however, it ceases to have meaning to man whose life is largely dominated by the secular.

## CONCLUSION

We now return to the point at which we have often found ourselves—to the affirmation that God alone gives ultimate meaning to history. Indeed, for the Christian to believe in God is to say that God is the basis of all that exists—the Ground of Being and thus of history.

It is God who reveals himself through history—dimly at first, later with more clarity (especially in the prophets), and with dramatic vividness in Jesus of Nazareth. It is the sovereign God who, because he is God and because we are finite, remains both unknown and known. We cannot finally solve the problem of evil or explain all the events of history; but we can avail ourselves of his concern, even his suffering love. God is present in history not only in past events and present experience, but also as a future hope. He who is Alpha is also Omega. In him all things hold together.

# Chapter VII

# THE INDIVIDUAL
# AND HISTORY

Is the individual a *pawn* of history or a *maker* of history?
Is he caught in a web of historical inevitability against which
he can struggle only to become more tightly entangled, or is
he partly or wholly free to make of life what he will? Is man
the master of his fate, as William Ernest Henley put it, or is
he only an incidental and insignificant illustration of a vast
complex of forces that determine the action of any separate
part? What can and should the Christian, individually, and
corporately in the church, do in an attempt to influence the
course of history?

The raising of these questions as a part of the present discussion is doubtless presumptuous, for they demand a much

97

more adequate consideration than can be given here. They involve, first of all, the question of freedom and determinism —what are the *possibilities* of man's changing the way things happen? Second, they involve questions about the *desirability* of the Christian's seeking to influence the larger society and, therefore, history. Nevertheless, we are obliged to look at the questions, if only to see how complicated man's situation is.

## FORMS OF DETERMINISM

Determinism is any variety of belief "that everything that happens is determined, is absolutely fixed by antecedent and contemporary conditions, and could not have happened differently."[1] Freedom implies at least some degree of choice, that happenings are not inevitable, but are to one degree or another the result of man's freedom.

We need to recognize at the outset that men are pretty well divided over the issue of freedom and determinism. In theological thought, for example, the issue traditionally has been stated as one of predestination or free will; and individual Christians have held tenaciously to one or the other position. The same diversity of belief is found among non-Christians. For example, Sigmund Freud was generally deterministic in his thinking, while Jean-Paul Sartre supports a rigorous and radical freedom.

So widespread is the belief that whatever happens is caused that almost any aspect of reality may be seen as the chief or sole determining factor in the course of life and history. Primitive man was usually a determinist and often a fatalist, though he did believe that under certain conditions he could alter the course of events. He saw some exterior cause for all events—a spirit or an ancestor, for example, sought to control his life. By performing certain ritualistic acts, he might persuade the outside force to bring good, rather than bad, to pass.

From the time of Sir Isaac Newton to the contemporary statement of the principle of indeterminism, modern science, on the other hand, generally has been deterministic in its

[1] From "Determinism," by John F. Dashiell, in *Encyclopedia Americana*, Vol. 9, p. 24.

belief in cause and effect within the natural conditions of reality. Science, in fact, can operate only when results can be predicted. If the natural or social scientist could not depend on the outcome of his experiments, he simply could not operate. Even those who recognize that not all effects can be predicted ("indeterminism") still must depend on the predictability of most outcomes. The principle of cause and effect in science has had tremendous influence on all areas of modern thought.

One form of determinism likely to be familiar to most of us is that of economic determinism, or the historical materialism articulated by Karl Marx. According to Marx, the economic factor determines all forms of production and distribution. Life proceeds on the basis of cause and effect in relationship to the way material existence is maintained. All other forms of life, therefore, must be made subsidiary to the economic.

Extreme *laissez-faire* capitalism also involves a kind of determinism. According to this economic theory, there are to be few if any controls on the economic process, since to exercise such controls is to upset the natural balance of the economic process. There is a kind of historical inevitability in a theory that insists, as this one does, that for man to regulate the economic process is to interfere with the "laws of nature and of history."

Geography also is seen as crucial in that climate, terrain, and similar factors often determine how a group of persons will live. History often is written as if political factors are the sufficient explanation of all events. Likewise, religious determinists from Augustine (perhaps from Paul) forward have insisted that God is the sufficient and direct cause of everything.

Many persons see the determining factors in events as residing in the individual. Freud, who was for the most part deterministic in his thinking, based many of his conclusions on biological factors operating in the individual. Other psychologists suggest a kind of "psychic determinism," the belief that a person's actions are determined by inner drives and the way in which he responds to forces brought to bear on these drives. In fact, many, perhaps most, psychologists, social scientists, and behavioral scientists tend toward some form of determinism. Much of the experimental work of the social scientist consists either of explaining the causes for present behavior or of predicting the course of future behavior.

Although only specialists are likely to hold rigidly any one kind of explanation for individual or group behavior, others tend to feel that, if one knew all the factors involved in some particular action, he would know precisely what to expect. Such knowledge would include unconscious as well as conscious motivations; it would involve personal feelings, biological urges and tendencies, sociological factors, and the like.

Thus we readily see that modern man can hardly escape the influence of determinism on his understanding both of his own life and of history. The variety of explanations of human and group behavior, however, indicates no universal understanding of, or support for, a single principle of causation.

For persons nurtured in an atmosphere generally emphasizing cause-and-effect relationship, the attempt to find explanations for all action is not only attractive; it is almost inevitable. Common sense and general information tell us why many things happen. If I am exposed to a disease germ or virus, I probably will become ill. If I overeat, I will be uncomfortable. If I hit a person, he may hit me back. If I follow the directions provided in a chemistry laboratory manual for some experiment, I will achieve the expected results.

With both common sense and scientific data to support him in his deterministic view, no wonder modern man often finds freedom a problem. His confusion is compounded by his living in a mass society where the individual often is lost in the crowd. Many people conclude, therefore, that there is no point in assuming responsibility in a mass society whose character is determined by forces beyond one's control.

## IS FREEDOM AN ILLUSION?

Given our understanding of the causes for many events and the possibility that such causes exist where they are not immediately evident, are we then to conclude that freedom is an illusion? Is man in both his personal and collective life a victim of historical processes over which he has no control?

One group of contemporary thinkers, some of whom are Christian and some of whom do not claim to be, strongly side with freedom. A varied lot in many ways, these are the existentialists. One idea they hold in common, however, is a radical belief in freedom and in the importance of man's asserting that freedom. Often opposed both to the preoccupation of modern man with science and to his succumbing to mass society, they speak out for the expression of man's individual selfhood in the face of all that seeks to control him.

The existentialist approach to freedom is neither theoretical nor experimental. That is, existentialists do not present a systematic theory of freedom in opposition, for example, to Marx's theory of economic determinism. Nor do they set out to confound the experiments of physical and social scientists and therefore prove an element of freedom and indeterminism in life. Rather, they call upon man to assert himself and thus prove himself to be free.

This approach to life, though not necessarily labeled *existentialist,* can be observed in those individuals who throughout history have taken circumstances in their hands and changed them: King David, Alexander the Great, Judas Maccabaeus, the Apostle Paul, Constantine, Pope Gregory the Great, Charlemagne, Martin Luther, John Wesley, George Washington, Henry David Thoreau, Abraham Lincoln, Pope John XXIII, Martin Luther King, Jr., and hundreds of less-well-known men and women.

Belief in freedom is strong also in the thought of specialists concerned with the human person in our time. Erich Fromm, a contemporary psychoanalyst, has a great deal to say about freedom, especially in his books *Escape From Freedom, Man for Himself,* and *The Heart of Man.* He recognizes in man the fear of freedom, since with freedom comes responsibility, from which man too often attempts to escape. "Positive freedom consists in the spontaneous activity of the total, integrated personality," he writes.[2]

David Riesman, a social psychologist and analyst, distin-

[2] From *Escape From Freedom,* by Erich Fromm (New York: Holt, Rinehart, and Winston, 1941) , p. 258.

guishes between other-directed and inner-directed persons. In his *The Lonely Crowd,* he finds our culture too often producing the other-directed person, one who takes his cues from those around him; but he hopes for more who are inner-directed, or who demonstrate their freedom from the domination of the crowd.

Psychologist Gordon Allport insists that operating within each person is a factor that cannot be explained on the basis of simple causes. He speaks of the "functional autonomy of motives"—that is, the development within the maturing person of that which is unique for that individual. A person becomes more than a reflection of his environment: he becomes himself. Although Allport does not use the word *self,* his *proprium* is equivalent to *self.* The proprium is that part of a person which, being distinctly his, gives him the capacity to act.[3]

What these theorists assert is borne out in human experience: *the impulse to be free is part of the basis for being free.* Freedom is a gift in the same way that speech and language are gifts. If, as most psychologists believe, the individual becomes a truly human being as a result of his interaction with culture, he is partly a product of his environment. Whether he is free or bound depends partly on whether he has been taught to be free.

We see an illustration of how the expectation of freedom or the lack of it operates in two broad cultural patterns. Generally, the religions of the East have emphasized that man is determined by factors over which he has no control. History is an endless repetition of cycles, and individuals have control over neither their own destinies nor that of the world. Existence is a series of reincarnations, a belief common to Hinduism and Buddhism; and man is bound to a series of meaningless rebirths except as he can escape from desire and be assimilated into the oversoul of the universe, or Nirvana. Although there are modern exceptions to this view, it has been the prevailing one in many parts of the East and has led to a willingness to accept one's fate without complaint.

[3] See *Becoming: Basic Considerations for a Psychology of Personality* (New Haven: Yale University Press, 1955) , pp. 41-55.

In the West, on the other hand, two factors have helped man assert his freedom: (1) the emphasis on man's potential and innate worth, found in Greek humanism and in Hebrew theistic humanism (man is created in the image of God and is of potential worth to God); (2) the linear view of history, which makes history a movement toward something and encourages man to participate in the ongoing process. Although man is not in control of the movement (for God is), he is able within limits to change its course.

In such an atmosphere, the practical expression of freedom in both religion and society was born. Therefore Paul could write "for freedom Christ has set us free; stand fast therefore, and do not submit again to a yoke of slavery" (Galatians 5:1). The framers of the Declaration of Independence, likewise, could declare that all men are endowed with the right to life, liberty, and the pursuit of happiness.

Our understanding of freedom and the possibility of man to influence history must rest finally on man himself and on his recognition of his ability to choose. The right to say no is especially cultivated in Western culture, which attempts to hold in tension freedom and control: The parent controls the young child, but allows him to say no. As the child more forcefully begins to assert himself, freedom begins. The conflict between control and freedom comes to focus when the adolescent openly rebels against adult authority. The conflict continues in both constructive and destructive ways as adults assert themselves. It may lead to conflict between groups, as in the 1960's, when the Afro-American began really to see the possibilities of freedom for himself. Freedom is costly for both man and God. In human affairs, it may lead to disorder; in the divine-human encounter, it provides the possibility for rebellion against God.

Belief in freedom is not primarily a speculative matter. It is, rather, based on the observation of man's disposition to act. It is observed in man's capacity to assume responsibility for himself and others, in the discrimination man makes between what he considers the better of alternatives. The potentiality for freedom is born in man, but the exercise of free-

103

dom and the accompanying disposition to choose must be encouraged and cultivated if man is to be truly free.

## LIMITS AND POSSIBILITIES OF FREEDOM

All of us experience the limits of freedom to some extent in our daily lives. Few of us have not felt at times, if not regularly, that we are caught in a web of circumstances over which we have no control. Family responsibilities mean that we must go daily to work. Decisions affecting our lives are made by employers, heads of state, school boards, city councils. Who has not at some time daydreamed about escaping to some island where one can be free from entangling relationships and unpleasant duties? Erich Fromm is right: the individual ordinarily has not a limitless number of alternatives, but only a few. Any extravagant view of man's freedom is, therefore, both sentimental and unrealistic.

The most profound limitation on freedom, however, has to do with the nature of man himself. Because man is man and not God, man is limited in his possibilities for action. No amount of historical development can overcome that limitation. Modern man is likely to overextend his capacities for both power and freedom, thus attempting to defy his creatureliness. "The tendency to overestimate the degree of increase of human freedom," writes Reinhold Niebuhr in *Faith and History*, "expresses itself most characteristically in the belief that the development of human capacities radically alters the human situation." The error about history "is the belief that man's ambiguous position as both a creature and a creator of history is gradually changed until he may, in the foreseeable future, become the unequivocal master of historical destiny." [4] Niebuhr sees this temptation of man to overestimate the degree of his freedom to act and create as the Christian understanding of the root of sin.

This is not the full story, however, for man does move forward. Niebuhr points to four categories of human capacity in which there has been historic growth, or, in the terms of our discussion, areas in which man has changed history. The most

[4] From *Faith and History*, pp. 70, 85, and *passim*.

obvious area is technological development, or man's power to utilize the forces of nature for his own ends. The second area is the whole range of human culture, including religion, philosophy, art, and social organization. The accumulation of both knowledge and experience in these areas makes growth possible. The third area is man's rational faculty, especially as growth in experience occurs. In a fourth area, Niebuhr recognizes more pretension than actualization—namely, man's relationship to the natural world. Although man has grown in many human relationships, he remains a creature of nature. The most obvious illustration of this fact is that man dies. He is also a heterosexual creature, finding his sexual fulfillment in the opposite sex. He likewise is born into a particular racial and cultural group and cannot escape from it.[5]

Though man is limited partly by who he is—a finite creature dependent upon the Creator for ultimate fulfillment—within their creaturehood, persons possess various levels of competency for action. Native endowment places upon some persons a greater responsibility than it does on others, endowment of intellectual ability, energy potential, creativity and imagination, even physical health. Although most of these qualities can be cultivated and improved, many persons are severely limited by inheritance while others are richly endowed by nature.

The capacity to act also depends on one's circumstances. The President of the United States obviously can do much more to shape history than can a secretary, across the Potomac in the Pentagon, whose responsibility is to type letters someone else dictates. The relatively few people who make up the power structure of a city—either because of their official positions or because of their influence on the decision-makers—determine what that city does about most important issues. What, in comparison, can a department-store salesman do about fair housing?

Yet both the secretary and the salesman do have a sphere of influence, however restricted. They have the power to vote and to influence a few other persons in the process. They can

[5] See *ibid.,* pp. 75, 76.

encourage friends and family to be open-minded. They can join a group working for improved legislation. What they can do is limited; but they *can* act, so that their influence, combined with that of like-minded people, can be greater than it at first appears.

It is, therefore, not possible to speak abstractly about "human possibilities," for the *person* with his *native endowment* in a *set of circumstances* must be taken into account. Individuals and their relationship to history range from the powerful to those of little or no influence. On one end of the continuum might be Winston Churchill, who both made history and interpreted it in his memoirs. On the other end of the continuum might be a mental patient, whose contact with reality has been completely lost. The rest of us would lie somewhere between these two extremes, depending upon the circumstances of our lives and the degree of intelligence, enthusiasm, energy, and drive with which we are able to meet those circumstances.

Individuals, then, are free to make history but are limited in their alternatives for doing so. Although one cannot be Winston Churchill, he need not be simply a pawn of history. One's decisions may be limited to a narrow sphere of activity, or they may be as broad as life itself. The point is not the range of one's action, but the faithfulness with which he bears his responsibility.

## CHRIST AND HISTORY

For the moment, let us leave the practical matter of how the individual relates to life and consider a theoretical model for interpreting the possibilities of such relationships. First I will point out, on the basis of Richard Niebuhr's thought, various possible relationships of both the church and the individual to culture or history. Later I will illustrate how one of the approaches—that which I consider most fruitful—can be implemented, especially by the individual, in relation to life and history.

*Christ Against Culture.* In *Christ and Culture,* one of the most influential theological works of recent years, Richard Niebuhr discusses five ways in which the church throughout its history has been related to culture. The five motifs or methods are designated in terms of the relationship of Christ and culture. Although they are applicable both to the corporate church and to the individual Christian, we shall apply them especially in the latter category. The next few pages of this chapter depend almost entirely upon Niebuhr's models.

The first of these motifs Niebuhr designates as "Christ Against Culture." Essentially this point of view rejects secular culture as evil and counsels the Christian to have nothing to do with "the world." It would mean in the realm of history that the Christian would be concerned with "holy history" but not with "general history," that he would see little relationship between God and history outside the church.

Two illustrations may help to delineate the nature of the position. Tertullian (160—ca. 220) advised Christians to shun all meaningful contacts with the pagan world—not only its pleasures but also its politics, philosophy, and art. He rejected the trend of his day, in which most Christian thinkers made correlations between Christian faith and the ideas of the Greek philosophers. Tertullian might well have had serious questions about the Roman culture of his day, but his complete rejection of it was extreme even for his time.

Then there are such groups as the Old Order Amish Mennonites of Pennsylvania, who form their own communities and refuse to wear modern clothing or use the technological developments of the twentieth century. Many such groups remain as part of the ordinary world, sending their children to public schools, but attempting to live according to their own understanding of Christian perfection.

There is, of course, a virtue in such persons and movements —what Niebuhr calls "the single-heartedness and sincerity of the great representatives of this type." [6] The Friends (or Quakers) are a prime illustration; though because of their concern for the society in which they live (without being

[6] From *Christ and Culture*, by H. Richard Niebuhr (New York: Harper & Brothers, 1951), pp. 65-66.

contaminated by it), they probably should not be included in this category.

Serious questions must be raised, however, concerning both the theological and practical adequacies of withdrawal from the world. Can a person really withdraw from society to the extent this position suggests? The pacifist, for example, cannot extricate himself completely from a war economy; for he, too, probably eats food grown by persons who support the war; or the money he spends may be used eventually to purchase weapons. The only possibility for nearly complete withdrawal is the way of the solitary mystic, cut off from almost all human contact. Yet even he is often forced to depend on others for his food.

Theologically, this extreme position lacks a sense of God's relationship to all of life. It emphasizes his redemptive action through Jesus Christ and the sustaining of the called community by the Spirit, but it fails to recognize the centrality of God's creation as the background for his redemption and his relationship to the whole of his creation. This position tends to deny, at least in practice, that God's creation is good and that his love is for the world, not just for the church. Although some of the secular theologians may go to extremes, they nevertheless are correct in reminding us of the weakness of any view that tries to restrict God's grace to a special group.

*The Christ of Culture.* The second position Niebuhr identifies is in some ways at the opposite pole from the first. Whereas the exponents of the first position seek to withdraw from the world, those of the second attempt to *identify* Christ and culture. The view is, on the one hand, an identification of the best elements of culture as Christian and, on the other, a selection from the total scope of Christian faith those elements one wishes to reproduce in culture.

A number of recent church movements have tended, in one way or another, to identify the best of culture with Christian faith. The "peace of mind" religion of the 1950's, for example, tended to identify the honest, dependable, charitable person with the Christian and to use God for the attainment of a state of self-approval and contentment. Early twentieth-century liberal theology, through its attempts to find meaningful ways of relating Christian faith to scientific knowledge, often forgot the elements of sin and judgment in original Christianity. The secular theologians discussed in a previous chapter are in danger of repeating a similar mistake in our time.

The most common tendency of this kind among churchmen today may be to identify being a Christian with being a good citizen. It is often difficult to discern any real contrast between the fellowship maintained in the community of faith and that found in the luncheon club, the garden club, or the PTA.

It should be clear by now that we face a bipolar situation when we consider these first two positions of Niebuhr's. It is not easy to maintain separateness and at the same time to affirm the goodness of creation and be related actively to the whole of that creation. Rejecting the world is often only one step from being sanctimonious; yet, as we noted in Chapter V, there are aspects of the world which must be rejected—its ghettos, its failure to deal constructively with the race issue, its injustices, its poverty. Perhaps the major question for both the church and the Christian is summarized in the title of Langdon Gilkey's book *How the Church Can Minister to the World Without Losing Itself.* Or in the words of the Gospel of John, How can the Christian be *in* but not *of* the world?

*Christ Above Culture.* Those who follow this motif attempt to establish the church as the ruler of culture and to influence secular life by legislation or, in the case of the medieval church, by the command of the king.

This position became generally accepted as that of the church regarding the world following the fall of the Roman Empire and the rather magnificent picking up of the pieces by Pope Gregory the Great. Gradually the church emerged as the primary stable force in culture, and—partly by default, partly because of some able popes—secured a fair amount of control over the whole culture. This great synthesis of church and culture—*Christendom* is the term often used to denote the synthesis—has continued to some extent until recent times, though its force was broken by the coming of the modern age, from the fifteenth century forward.

Not only has the Roman Catholic Church maintained this position until recently, with a tendency to relinquish it since Vatican II; many Protestant groups also, often without realizing what they were doing, have held this basic attitude toward the world. The tendency for the public schools in the United States to reflect a generally Protestant attitude stems partly from the fact that, in colonial New England, the church elders, the town rulers, and the school board were one and the same group—a kind of "divine commonwealth."

First because of developing religious pluralism and later because of the increasing secularization of life, the church's domination of education and legislation has decreased considerably. Recent decisions of the Supreme Court in regard to religion and public education led one Jewish rabbi to say, "I'm glad that the public schools are ceasing to be Protestant parochial schools." Gradually, also, laws imposed on the whole society by some religious groups—for example, those pertaining to contraception and to the closing of all businesses on Sunday—are being removed.

Niebuhr's third position, nevertheless, is an attractive one to many Christians, especially to those who feel that it is important to bring the influence of Christianity to bear on all of culture. If, as Niebuhr points out, we take seriously our belief that God ought to be related to all men, we will try to find means of implementing that belief. In spite of the undesirability, therefore, of maintaining church control over education, the search for some unifying principle in life still shows up among those concerned with the relationship of religion and public education. Since the question concerns what the center of education is to be, the justifiable fear is that if Christian faith is not that center, some other faith will be. The danger, according to theologian Harvey Cox and others, is that the process of true secularization will be thwarted by the establishment of a new religion of secularism, a planned and active support of a nontheistic interpretation of life.

Remembering instances in history when the church has controlled society and has used this control to seek uniformity, one can scarcely be attracted to this position. Roman Catholics have persecuted Protestants; Protestants have persecuted

Roman Catholics and other Protestants; and both groups have persecuted Jews. Further, there is always the temptation, as Niebuhr indicates, to try to make permanent a given cultural form that has been related to the Christian faith. For example, Gothic architecture became so identified with the proper form for a church building that it has been difficult for new patterns in church architecture to develop.

There is, of course, the further problem, especially in societies as culturally pluralistic as those of the United States and Canada, of determining the particular forms a synthesis of religion and culture will assume. Thus the third motif does not seem acceptable as a viable means of relating the gospel to history.

*Christ and Culture in Paradox.* Niebuhr's fourth position is a both/and motif—the attempt to keep the sinful world and the church in tension, to live in the world but not be of it. Martin Luther is the most noted proponent of the position, which is not easy to state. In an oversimplified form, it means that the absolute demands of living in obedience to Christ are seen in radical contrast with the demands of living in the world. The Christian is to live responsibly in this world, but he must recognize the relative nature of many of his decisions.

Luther was especially sensitive to the demands placed upon the Christian who is responsible for others—for example, for the person who is husband and father. Because such a person is an instrument by which God supplies daily food to children, he must work for money, rather than just for the glory of God; and he may even be required to defend himself and others against the thief or other foe. When a person is responsible only for himself, he can carry out the absolute demands of Christ; where he is responsible for others, what he must do for their welfare often is in conflict with absolute Christian love. For example, a father who is a clerk in a store may be asked to lie about the merchandise he sells.

To a great extent, this fourth position is a true picture of life. Unfortunately, this position can be used as an excuse for not being responsible in culture. The confessing church in Germany, formed in the midst of World War II by such men as Dietrich Bonhoeffer, accepted as a judgment against the German church the fact that it had not resisted soon enough the inroads of Hitler. It had not done so because the church believed that it was not to interfere in those things which belonged to Caesar. This position may be seen vividly in the objection of many American churchmen to the church's involvement in socio-economic-political matters.

This position is a dangerous one. On the other hand, it must be taken seriously as the beginning point for understanding the relationship of Christ and culture or history. In its radical recognition of the sinfulness both of man individually and of culture generally, it speaks to those who would too easily identify the best of culture with Christian faith ("Christ of culture"). In its insistence that life must be lived in the world, the position cautions those who would withdraw from the world ("Christ against culture"). In its recognition of the temporal nature of all of man's achievement, it speaks to those who would form a synthesis of Christ and culture by identifying imperfectly Christianized forms with the absolute ("Christ of culture").

In spite of its realism about life and history, however, this position is incomplete. It allows man to excuse himself too easily for not taking his faith seriously. It therefore points to the need for something more, and this added dimension is found in a fifth position.

## CHRIST, THE TRANSFORMER OF CULTURE

Those who hold to Niebuhr's fourth position and who therefore recognize the importance of keeping the world and faith in tension are pessimistic about culture and history. The conversionists, of his fifth position, generally agree with the realistic picture these dualists paint of culture and history; but conversionists are more hopeful about the possibilities within history. They believe, writes Niebuhr, that culture "is under God's sovereign rule, and that the Christian must carry on cultural work in obedience to the Lord. For the conversionist, history is the story of God's mighty deeds and of man's responses to them." [7]

The position maintained in previous chapters of this book is essentially Niebuhr's fifth motif. By my insistence that all of life and history must be recognized as the realm of God's activity, I have supported the view that the Christian must be concerned with what happens in all of life. Implied in this approach to God's universal concern for life is also the assumption that man must act responsibly in all of life. A view of the kingdom of God that calls for its relationship to the whole of life and history and includes the belief that man can perform "signs of the Kingdom" also points to the position Niebuhr designates as "Christ the transformer of culture."

The precise means by which man individually and the church corporately transform history are yet to be considered. For the time being, we must only assert that those who support Niebuhr's fifth position must be about the business of dealing with the problems of society and history. In so doing, they will deal, among other things, with such issues as race, poverty, injustice, and world order. In working on such matters, they invariably will come into conflict with some church members as well as with persons outside the church.

This conflict will be especially acute between the conversionists and those who wish to prevent change. This is essentially the desire of the reactionary (as opposed to the true conservative, who desires to conserve the best from the past while not opposing necessary change). The reactionary is likely to wish not only to stop the processes of history, but also to return to some former period of history, usually to what he imagines to be the simpler life of the nineteenth century. Into day's fast-moving world, however, history is not likely to be stopped, much less turned back.

Concerned Christians, therefore, must find ways by which they can be instruments of transformation, even if for only some small part of history. If the point of view of this chapter is valid, individuals need not be victims of history: they may be change-agents. This means that they will be realistic about

[7] *Ibid.*, p. 195.

existing possibilities for action and that they will select genuine alternatives for action. It means, also, that they will act.

The model I have chosen by which the Christian can understand his responsibility to work actively within the historical process neither involves impossible demands nor allows inaction. It takes full account of personal gifts and different circumstances. Although it does not prescribe a particular *kind* of action, it describes Christian action in terms of the commandment to love and be concerned for one's neighbor. The outcome of such action cannot be predicted, for ultimately it is in God's hands. The important thing is that the possibility of change be affirmed and the demand for active involvement in history be upheld.

## AN APPROACH TO METHODOLOGY

It is within neither the scope nor the range of this chapter to present a detailed approach to the transformation of culture and the changing of history. All that is here possible is to suggest some general approaches to a complicated subject. In the following chapter, we shall consider specifically ways of facing five recurring problems of history.

One of the first questions the Christian must face in regard to history is whether the church should act on the issues of culture and history as a body—that is, whether corporate action is either desirable or possible. Social ethicist Gayraud Wilmore is quite clear on the point: either the church must act as a body, or it cannot hope to influence the social structures of our time. He points out that God has used individuals to change the world, but believes that corporate action is needed today.

> By corporate action, we refer simply to "acting as a body." This may involve the official, authorized action of a congregation; or action by a group of churches or by that delegated body that is able to act in their behalf. It will be clear, therefore, that by corporate action we mean to imply action as an organized power group which may not be able to deliver all that it promises in the way of effective power, but which has,

nevertheless, some of the resources and some of the institutional weight of a corporate entity behind it.[8]

For some, this approach will be too much like the "Christ above culture" motif. Others will be afraid of such action or will disagree with it, rationalizing that the church has no business being involved in such matters. True, there may be a difference between the church as a power group engaging in social action and individuals being led by the church to participate in reforms. But this argument must be kept on the methodological, rather than the principle, level; for all we have said thus far points to the fact that the gospel is, by its very nature, concerned with all of life. Those who seek to put the gospel into effect must deal with the issues of life and history, whatever those issues are.

Our purpose in this chapter, however, is to consider the *individual* and history. We may, therefore, leave largely unanswered the question concerning corporate action and look, instead, at how individuals may act responsibly in the ongoing processes of life and history.

First, the individual may in some measure influence history through faithful obedience to his vocation as an individual Christian, that vocation being his call to serve God in all he is and does—in daily work, play and leisure, family life, the church, relationships with neighbors, politics, community life, and all other areas where persons live and move and have their being.

Let us again contrast the possibilities for a decision-maker —say, a city councilman—and a salesman who sells him a pair of shoes. The responsibility of the councilman is obviously considerable, for his decisions regularly affect the life and destiny of the citizens of his city. Whether he acts responsibly with regard to substandard housing may be the factor that determines both the welfare of the children of those who live under substandard conditions and whether the city will be torn by racial strife. His decision not to provide parks and

[8] From *The Secular Relevance of the Church,* by Gayraud S. Wilmore, pp. 53-54.

recreation centers for youth may lead young people into trouble and thus increase the incidence of juvenile delinquency. The failure to deal with the health problems of one portion of the city not only jeopardizes the physical welfare of those who live there; it may lead to similar problems throughout the city. The willingness of such a person to act responsibly on behalf of the total populace literally can change the course of the city's history.

The shoe salesman can make no such far-reaching decisions. He does have within his power, however, decisions which affect his immediate family. They are likely to be a series of small decisions the results of which contribute either to the building of stable character within his children or to its destruction. He has the right and responsibility, along with his neighbors, to vote intelligently. If his time allows, he may serve as a tutor and help a culturally deprived child remain in school. He may extend himself to other parts of the world as he participates in a drive to raise money for UNICEF.

Frederick Wentz, president of Hamma School of Theology, illustrates the impact of individuals on their immediate surroundings, and in some instances beyond, in the case studies included in *My Job and My Faith*. One is the story of a farmer, Richard C. Waybright, who writes: "So I felt a special call to do everything possible in my small corner of the earth to set a modest example of helping to provide food for the world by helping to improve the facilities and methods of the food producers." [9] While utilizing the changes in food production so that one man can now do what ten men could do twenty years ago, Mr. Waybright also attempts to make it possible for all those who work on his farms to enjoy the fruits of intellectual and artistic culture.

A second illustration comes from the life of a woman who, after her husband's death, supported five children by doing domestic work. She confided to Dr. Wentz that she had never thought of her work in relation to her Christian faith, but she did say:

[9] From *My Job and My Faith*, Frederick K. Wentz, ed. (Nashville: Abingdon Press, 1967), pp. 125-126.

There's a satisfaction in doing a thorough job of cleaning a floor, a room, a whole house. . . . I guess an important part of it is that people come to trust me. . . . Maybe at 9 A.M. the wife explains that she must take the children shopping in Baltimore, and at noon her husband rushes in and out on his way to the golf course, leaving me taxi money. All day I work hard so that she'll be pleased with the clean house when she gets back. And I figure I work harder than usual (even though I get paid by the hour) to prove something to myself (page 153).

Most persons are not going to work wonders in the historical process by the faithful answering of their call to be responsible before God and neighbor. Yet it is through such humble work that much of the world's life is carried on. However small one man's influence may seem to be in contrast to the broad sweep of history, he is called to faithful participation in history-making in those realms of his personal existence where he has some influence.

The second way in which the individual participates in history-making is by his work through groups, both in and out of the church. Many persons have become dissatisfied with the slow manner in which most church groups move, to the point that they despair of their effectiveness in the larger world. Nor are church groups necessarily the most effective means for carrying on many kinds of social action, or history-making. So the person who wants to participate in the transformation of culture, and thus of history, may find himself doing his most effective work through nonchurch groups.

Three examples will illustrate the point. Suppose a community becomes concerned with juvenile delinquency. The most effective approach to the matter will probably be a community-wide one, in which church people participate and in which the organized church plays its part. Since the problem is not confined to any one part of the community, it is almost certain that a group uniting people from many and varied traditions of the community will be the most effective.

A second illustration is found in the movement for justice and equality for the Afro-American in the total society of the

117

United States in the 1960's. I would not deny that the churches, both white and Afro-American but especially the latter, played an important role in preparing individuals for the action of the late 1950's and 1960's. I am even more convinced that there came a time when the churches, especially the predominantly white ones, could not operate effectively in the field. Individual clergymen and laymen could, but the leadership of and participation in the movement of necessity had to be on a broader basis.

A third illustration may be briefly noted—the approach of the churches to the involvement of the United States in the Vietnam War in the 1960's. Increasingly in 1966 and 1967, opposition to the indefinite continuation of participation grew, while the feelings of those who favored the policies being pursued or approved of even more escalation also became more intense. The point here is only this: churches were as divided over the issue as was the nation. Church groups did to some extent participate in the debate; but the more effective means of dealing with the issue, regardless of which side a person took, was obviously by political action and other means outside the structures of the church.

We might continue illustrating the many corporate problems facing us today in history and thus show that the individual will feel lost if he remains a lone individual facing such problems. As a participant in a carefully chosen group, however, he at least can feel that he is effecting some small measure of change in his complex world.

## CONCLUSION

We began this chapter by raising questions concerning the individual's being a change-agent in, rather than a victim or a pawn of, history. We have seen the need to be realistic concerning the limits of man's freedom and of his ability to participate meaningfully in the broad sweep of history. Some persons are able to be more effective than others, depending upon their gifts and the circumstances of their lives. But the significant thing is that each person is called to act responsibly in all the realms of his calling.

118

# Chapter VIII

# RECURRING PROBLEMS IN HISTORY

A serious appraisal of world history can easily lead to the conclusion that the cyclical version of the historical process is right, after all. As we read the pages from the past, we find a seemingly recurring round of problems which, though possessing a peculiar character according to various periods of time, demonstrate a discouraging similarity.

Arnold J. Toynbee's analysis of the rise and fall of civilizations in his ten-volume *A Study of History* indicates at least elements of similarity in the historical process with regard to the rise and fall of cultures. Considering the long succession of wars in human history, beginning with conflicts between tribes and extending through the twentieth-century global conflicts, one can only marvel at man's unwillingness to learn from the past. As one surveys the large areas of racial strife in the world today, one can only shake his head in amazement at man's continuing blindness. Toynbee's conclusion to his study of history is somewhat optimistic; one might just as easily, however, be led to a pessimistic one.

Without some view, however dim, of man's achievements within history, we would be led almost inevitably to despair. Chapter VII sought to present a realistic but somewhat hopeful picture of the possibilities of human freedom and of man's accomplishments. The limitations of man were frankly faced—indeed, some would say they were emphasized too much. Man's possibilities were also examined, with the cautious conclusion that man can change history, though in a way limited both by his native endowment and by the circumstances of his life.

We can no longer, I believe, appraise life with the extravagant optimism characteristic of both the social scientist and the general public prior to World War I and the depression of 1929. Social reformers of those days, both in and outside the church, seriously believed that the recurring problems of mankind could be solved. I remember now, with some embarrassment, that while I was in seminary in the late 1930's, I wondered what man would do when he no longer had social problems on which to work! The prevailing mood of early twentieth-century life can be summarized in the popular slogan of the French psychotherapist Émil Coué: "Day by day, in every way, I am getting better and better."

While we cannot face the world and history with the optimism characteristic of the early part of this century, we can recognize both the possibilities and the responsibilities of the Christian man to work with and through the historical process to effect desirable change. A model for dealing responsibly with life was presented in the previous chapter.

Near the end of Chapter VII, general suggestions were made with respect to how the Christian can act responsibly in society and thus participate in history-making. Although these suggestions apply particularly to those kinds of situations over which we have at least some degree of direct control, they are appropriate in different ways for other types of situations.

We may work directly on a problem such as juvenile delinquency or a school election. We work indirectly on a matter such as world order by participating, for example, in the United Nations Association.

This chapter is concerned with five recurring problem areas of history. The first two, *conflict* and *power,* cannot be specifically delineated as problems; rather, they have to do with conditions of human existence that issue in problems. *Poverty* and *ethnic divisions,* two other of the five areas, directly involve practical issues which, though not the same under all conditions, nevertheless retain many of the same characteristics from one age to another. The fifth problem—that of *political freedom*—is especially a modern concern in that it has come to some degree of fruition during the last two centuries, though it has its roots in the beginnings of human community. Other problems might have been chosen, though I believe these are representative. These five are treated briefly and in summary only.

The concerns of this chapter are presented from the perspective of the convictions supported in Chapter VII—namely, that the Christian can help shape history in at least some limited sense and that he has the responsibility for doing so. Underlying the chapter is the conviction, stated especially in Chapter V, that the entire range of the created order is God's concern and is therefore the concern of the Christian—politics, economic life, world order, and the lot. If God loves the world (John 3:16), then his human children are called to implement that love in concrete ways in the time of their lives.

## CONFLICT

"History," writes Kenneth E. Boulding, contemporary sociologist and perceptive social analyst, "is largely the record of conflict." [1] Conflict occurs in the most intimate relationships of life (for example, those between husband-wife, parent-child), at the same time including the more impersonal as-

---

[1] From *Conflict and Defense: A General Theory,* by Kenneth E. Boulding (New York: Harper Torchbooks, 1962, 1963), p. 1. The material in this section is greatly dependent on Boulding's views.

pects of human existence, such as relationships between nation-states.

*The Meaning of Conflict.* Boulding suggests four concepts common to an understanding of conflict. First there is the *party,* a term he uses to designate a "behavior unit" or any person or group capable of assuming a variety of positions on a subject while retaining its or his identity. A party may be a single person, a nation, or any aggregate between these extremes. The second concept Boulding sets forth is *behavior space,* or the set of future positions the party may take—that is, the way the party may be expected to act.

Third, there is *competition,* a condition arising when the potential behavior spaces or types of reaction of any two parties are incompatible. Competition in its broadest interpretation is nothing more than disagreement—that is, the occupying of two different positions by two persons or groups whose paths cross. *Conflict,* the fourth concept, arises whenever the parties are aware of the competition of their future positions, when "each party wishes to occupy a position that is incompatible with the wishes of the other" (page 5).

Robert Ardrey, playwright turned anthropologist and naturalist, presents a fascinating theory concerning the animal origins of conflict. In *The Territorial Imperative,* published in 1966 and subtitled "A Personal Inquiry into the Animal Origins of Property and Nations," he develops the theory that the basis for conflict between birds and animals of the same species lies in their competition for living space or territory. They stake out their territory, he contends, and fight any creature of the same species that encroaches on the territory. I shall not attempt to say whether Ardrey is right or wrong, though his theory points to deep-rooted conflict in the biological make-up of man.

*Solving Conflict.* What should be the attitude of the Christian man toward conflict, and how should he deal with it? Boulding's three-part approach to methods of dealing with conflict is helpful here: *avoidance, conquest,* and *procedural resolution,* or some form of reconciliation or compromise (pages 310-311 and following).

Perhaps the most common approach to conflict by the church, especially in our time, is *the attempt to avoid conflict.* Many pastors, for example, fear nothing more than that someone might "rock the boat," meaning that someone might bring the disagreement and conflict in a congregation into the open. They forget the warning of Jeremiah as he sought to stir up his people to the dangers of complacency:

> They have healed the wound of my people lightly,
>     saying, "Peace, peace,"
> when there is no peace. (Jeremiah 6:14 and 8:11)

They forget also the word of Jesus, "Do not think that I have come to bring peace on earth; I have not come to bring peace, but a sword" (Matthew 10:34; see also Luke 12:51-53).

The same attempt to avoid conflict also often has characterized the relationship of the church and the individual Christian to the problems of the world. Conflict has been avoided because either the individual or the group did not wish to get involved or because they saw no responsibility for dealing with the unsavory situations of life.

This is not to suggest that one necessarily ought to go looking for trouble (though everyone knows situations of complacency in which it would be well for someone deliberately to stir up something). Ordinarily enough, disagreement already exists if it can but be brought into the open. Where conflicts do exist, they cannot be solved by default: something has to be done, and this means openly facing the conflict.

The following types of situations are examples of ones in which the Christian man or a Christian group may need to take the initiative both in making the conflict open and, at the same time, in dealing with it: a community where Negroes live in ghetto conditions and where the community power structure insists there is no problem; a city in which one power group has dominated the school board with its primary concerns being to keep taxes low and discourage educational innovation; a PTA that is being infiltrated by the radical right; an organization in a similar danger from the radical left; a community with no concern about its lack of recreational facilities for young people.

Although there is likely to be incipient conflict in any situation, complacency may have hidden it. A situation of complacency requires that someone (or perhaps some event) upset the equilibrium that has led to complacency. To be sure, the person who decides to try to change the situation must be prepared to face certain problems: one's job may be put in jeopardy, for example, so that one has to decide between allowing some evil to continue and losing his livelihood. Some people are naturally even tempered and do not find it easy to lead a fight; others do not have the ability to secure a response from others. Most people will, therefore, find themselves participating in a movement with others, rather than providing leadership for it. In any case, avoiding conflict is not the answer.

*Conquest,* especially in the form of war, also has been a common way of solving conflict. Not all conquest, of course, is on the part of the aggressor; for if one party to a conflict conquers the other, regardless of who initiated the conflict, this method of solving conflict has been utilized.

Conquest operates, however, not just in situations involving war. Family quarrels get nowhere when one person is intent on "having the last word" and thereby conquering the other. Parents, it is true, must exercise discipline in conflict situations with their children; but discipline is not identical with conquest.

Situations of internecine church conflict often are kept alive —even started—because one side is determined to win over another. Conquest usually means that the conflict is not really solved, however, unless there is some kind of reconciling follow-up. The total victory of the Allied Forces over both Germany and Japan in World War II was followed by a rather remarkable effort at rehabilitation of the two countries by the Allies, so that what could have been a hopelessly vindictive situation became constructive—at least in many ways.

Should the church seek to conquer the world in its conflicts with culture? That is essentially the meaning of the

"Christ above culture" motif considered in Chapter VII. When this motif is followed, the church seeks to secure by legislation, or by other coercive means, what it wishes to see happen in society. Two problems were indicated when this motif was considered in Chapter VII: First, the cultural pluralism of such nations as the United States and Canada makes such legislation virtually impossible even if it might be desirable. Although Christian positions will often coincide with those of the state (for example, laws against murder), common consent by the general population is the necessary basis for law. Second, when such action is taken, there is always the temptation to equate legal action with the absolute Christian law of love and therefore to absolutize the law.

We are left with the third of Boulding's possible approaches to the solving of conflict—namely, the *procedural resolution* of conflict, involving reconciliation and compromise. "In procedural resolution," writes Boulding, "the parties have to stay together and live with each other; conflict, in general, may not be resolved permanently insofar as the parties continue to exist in contact, but particular conflicts may be resolved simply in the sense that they come to an end as social systems and are replaced by other conflicts and other systems." [2]

Where reconciliation is possible, this position is clearly in harmony with Christian faith. (See Paul's summary of that faith in terms of reconciliation in 2 Corinthians 5:17-20.) Since reconciliation involves, as Boulding says, modifications in the images both parties to the conflict have of one another, this type of resolution implies that something has happened to both of the persons or groups involved.

Because of a traditional absolutist tendency in Christian ethics, however, the idea of *compromise* seems less desirable to many Christians. There is a fear that compromise means giving up one's principles; and, of course, there *is* always the danger that the compromise position will become identified as the normative. Yet in all human situations, including the interior life of the organized church, absolutist positions are

[2] *Ibid.*, pp. 390-391.

125

difficult to maintain without sacrificing human values. One may, in fact, be completely false to human persons in his attempt to be true to his principles. Jesus' statement "The sabbath was made for man, not man for the sabbath . . ." is appropriate at this point (Mark 2:27).

What is said here regarding the solving of conflict is applicable inside the institutional church; it is appropriate also to the larger society. One of the responsibilities of the Christian, we have already seen, may be to stir up conflict when complacency has covered up wrongs festering beneath the surface. It is not enough that he stop at this point, however: he ought also to seek means of bringing about reconciliation. Through its teaching ministry, the church can encourage people in reconciliation and provide training for them in exercising the role. Part of this training will concern the necessity of compromise itself—help in recognizing that desions are usually some shade of gray, rather than black or white.

*War as the Result of Conflict.* The most devastating result of conflict, especially in our time, is war, or the attempt to solve conflict between nations through armed combat. After two global wars, the concept of limited war (as represented by the wars in Korea and Vietnam) has been accepted by many nations of the world. Whether or not modern warfare can be thus confined remains to be seen, of course.

What should be the Christian attitude toward war? There is the absolute pacifist position—the refusal on the basis of conscience to support any war. This position has often been associated with a perfectionist ethic—that is, the refusal to have anything to do with less-than-perfect situations. Some pacifists today, however, are pragmatic in their orientation— that is, they have decided that war is a greater evil than any other possibility.

On the opposite extreme from pacifism is the position that affirms the inevitability if not the desirability of war, a position that supports any war in which one's country is involved. Between these two extremes are various relative positions, such as support of limited war in an attempt to avoid all-out war.

The opposition to the Vietnam war in the United States in the late 1960's indicated that more and more people refuse to accept the concept of inevitable war and insist, instead, upon the right of the individual to protest what seem to be unjust wars.

One note of hope may be sounded among the many discouraging aspects of international conflict. This is the fact that the rise of the nation-state in the world from the late Middle Ages forward has created larger and larger areas where an alternative to war has been found. While civil war is always a threat where there is deep injustice and suppression of any group, it is not now common except in the new nations of Asia and Africa. Indeed, what has happened is that power blocs tend to be formed (such as the Allied Forces and the Axis Powers of World War II). Many had hoped that the United Nations could accomplish more in the way of peacefully solving conflict than it has done, though its accomplishments have not been negligible. Certainly, the strengthening of the United Nations to the end of solving conflict on a worldwide basis remains one of the crucial but only partly solved problems of our time.

Conflict is inevitable: the Christian understanding of life accepts this fact as a part of man's estranged condition (or sin). But this does not imply that means cannot be found for peacefully solving conflict. The church and the individual Christian are called to work actively toward the development of such means on all levels of human relationship.

## POWER

Power, of course, is not necessarily a problem, though its abuse leads to problems. Power itself is neutral; its use is the crucial matter. Indeed, power may be defined simply as the ability to get things done. The purpose of some units of power may be to operate a factory or to drive an automobile, while other power seeks to effect changes in the structure of a city government or a school system. We are, naturally, concerned with the power for accomplishment in the area of human relationships.

*The Broadening of Power.* The development of modern life has been partly a matter of broadening the base for decision-making and for carrying out decisions. In primitive life, the chief, or perhaps the priest, held power over his tribe. Centralized power was the rule rather than the exception in civil organization until recent times. Even the first milestone in English democratic history, the granting of the Magna Carta by King John in 1215, dispersed power only to the nobility, though the charter served as the basis for the later granting of rights to a larger segment of the population.

The eighteenth century, with the French and the American revolutionary wars and the peaceful revolution in Great Britain, witnessed the continuing dispersion of power. The extension of suffrage in the nineteenth and twentieth centuries has continued to broaden the base of power. At the same time, the power of the voluntary group has been increasing, so that now one of the primary sources of power, in the United States especially, is the voluntary association.

Third only to government and business in their power to get things done, these voluntary groups include the National Association of Manufacturers, the AFL-CIO, the League of Women Voters, the political parties, the John Birch Society, various health and welfare organizations—up to some 250,000 groups. Some such groups are concerned chiefly with the welfare of those who constitute the organization; others are concerned with the general welfare or with the welfare of persons outside as well as inside the group. A few are politically left wing; some are right wing; some, conservative; some, liberal; others, middle of the road.

*The Church and the Corporate Use of Power.* Church members constitute a considerable bloc of the membership of these associations, the churches themselves constituting one kind of such voluntary institutions. Potentially the churches are a considerable power bloc, but they usually do not act as such. Many churchmen accept as normative that churches should *not* seek to exert influence in the secular world. This point of view leads to criticism of both the separate denominations and the councils of churches when they seek by resolution or otherwise to exert influence in community, state, or nation.

Generally Protestantism is confused about its responsibility in the use of power. As Gayraud Wilmore puts it:

> When one considers the Protestant indecision about its cultural role, its long-standing disinclination to resort to secular means to achieve goals upon which there may be considerable agreement, and the great difficulty the churches have in reaching that agreement and legitimizing its expression in public pronouncement and action, the result is a picture of the stalemate in which Protestantism stands with respect to increasing its influence in the American power structure.[3]

Wilmore goes on to state his belief that the church should act corporately in bringing its influence to bear on the culture; that such action, if anything is to be done, involves the use of power. We noted in the discussion of conflict that the church's resolution of problems or concerns by conquest is close to, if not identical with, the "Christ above culture" motif considered in Chapter VII. The use of power is not the same as conquest, however, unless that power is used without due consideration of the rights of others. That there are both difficulties and dangers in the use of power by the organized church is clear—difficulties because of the lack of agreement among church members on specific issues; dangers because of the temptation of the church, as of other groups, to abuse its power.

One model for the use of power by a parish may be found in the work of the East Harlem Protestant Parish, consisting of several churches operating as one parish since the mid-1940's in one of the worst slums of New York City. The pattern followed has been to unite the forces of the parish—church staffs, lay members, and other concerned persons in the community—in bringing pressure to bring about some desired action. Action has effected such things as the following: repairs and heat for rotting tenement houses; regulation of police brutality; and municipal treatment for drug addicts. The

[3] From *The Secular Relevance of the Church*, by Gayraud S. Wilmore, p. 46.

method used to achieve action has been to marshall evidence, go as a group to the person or group responsible for dealing with the problem, and continue to press for something to be done.

One incident involved a landlord who installed a thermostat in his apartment building, according to city ordinance, but who placed it near the furnace and set it at 50 degrees! The tenants protested to the landlord and were threatened with eviction. One of the parish ministers helped the tenants buy thermometers which they placed in their apartments and from which they took hourly readings over a twenty-four-hour period. Temperature charts were presented to a city inspector; the landlord was taken to court and fined; and the temperature in the building rose.[4]

*The Individual and the Use of Power.* In Chapter VII, a great deal was made of the responsibility of the individual in the transformation of culture. In the great accomplishments of past cultures, some individual—the pharaoh, the king, a Moses, a Caesar, a Charlemagne—usually assumed leadership for a group. Modern times still have their charismatic leaders —the Churchills, the Adenauers, the Martin Luther Kings; but in a culture so widely represented by power groups as is today's, the ordinary individual exercises his influence most effectively, perhaps, as a part of one or more groups. This point was made in the previous chapter as we considered ways in which the individual can be a change-agent.

The businessman participates in the NAM, the laborer in the AFL-CIO. The housewife or professional woman joins the League of Women Voters; the parent, the PTA. A person can find a group to represent almost any cause in which he believes; and it may be, as we saw in Chapter VII, that to participate in such secular organizations is a more effective means for promoting the common good than trying to act through organized church groups. Certainly this is the case in those areas where there is a group whose purpose approximates a person's interpretation of his Christian responsibility.

[4] See *Come Out the Wilderness*, by Bruce Kenrick (New York: Harper & Row, 1962), for the story of the East Harlem Protestant Parish.

In any case, we must not reject the use of power as somehow less than Christian. The church must see power as a necessary ingredient of the historical process and use it wisely. At the same time, it must provide more adequate guidance to its members in their attitudes toward and their use of power.

## POVERTY

The first point to be made with respect to poverty is the difficulty of determining who is to be included in that category. One analyst of poverty in the United States adopts a yearly income of between $3,000 and $3,500 for a family of four as the cut-off point, and thus estimates that there are between 40,000,000 and 50,000,000 people living in poverty.[5] A salary of $3,000 a year, on the other hand, is an unbelievable amount of income to the poor in most of the underdeveloped nations of the world. Further, poverty varies with respect to different periods of history. Thus an analysis of the meaning of poverty depends upon what is the decent living expectation for a given part of the world at a given period of time.

Poverty of recent derivation is more manageable than that which is long standing. Indeed, there is some reason for distinguishing between the poor and the poverty-stricken. For example, my family were quite poor, pioneer West Texas farmers. I *do not* consider them poverty *stricken,* however; for they were ambitious, especially for their children. A person may have little of the goods of the world and still maintain his self-respect. A family on relief may spend more money than one in which there is an earner; but if the situation of the family on relief is of long standing, perhaps reflecting a way of life inherited from parents and even grandparents, it may be almost hopelessly ensnared in the vicious circle of poverty. What such a family needs most is to see the possibility of another kind of life.

Whatever one's definition of poverty, it is one of the recurring problems of history. It is characterized by hunger, filth, disease, early death, and the lack of a chance to live a

[5] See *The Other America: Poverty in the United States,* by Michael Harrington (New York: The Macmillan Company, 1962), pp. 182-183.

meaningful life. With the population of the world increasing at an alarming rate and with vast segments of the world's population not willing to recognize that the indiscriminate breeding of children is no longer desirable, one wonders what the future may hold. Indeed, many people believe that the most alarming problem the world faces is not war but over-population. Increased population is sure to lead to increased poverty unless there is a drastic increase in the world's food supply and an accompanying improvement of the means of distribution of the world's goods.

*Attempts to Alleviate Poverty.* Until very recent times, at-tempts to relieve the sufferings of poverty have been con-fined largely to gifts to persons in need. The church early began the task of relieving the poverty of its own members. (See Acts 6:1; Acts 24:17; and 1 Corinthians 16:1.) After Constantine, the church broadened its concern to include nonchurch members; but its interest was in the alleviation of suffering, not in the healing of social wrongs.[6] Throughout the Middle Ages, the church was the principal or only agency helping the poor; and she has continued to hold this distinc-tion until fairly recent times.

During the past seventy-five years, the work of organized charity has increasingly been assumed by private social agen-cies and by local, state, and national governments. Private nonchurch agencies include Family Service, the Red Cross, Travelers Aid, and the like. There are such services as aid to dependent children, subsistence payments for the very poor, health services, and the like on a county level. States provide old-age assistance and health services. More recently, the federal government has become interested in dealing with the poor.

Most past efforts in regard to poverty have been remedial—the providing of food, clothing, medical aid, and the like for people who cannot afford such services. As one of my theology professors put it some years ago, the church has been more

[6] See *The Social Teachings of the Christian Churches*, by Ernst Troeltsch, Olive Wyon, tr. (New York: Harper & Brothers, 1960), Vol. I, p. 134.

active in providing an ambulance at the bottom of a cliff to take maimed people to the hospital than it has been in building a fence to keep them from falling off. This attitude has generally prevailed in society as a whole.

We have often assumed that poverty is a temporary condition and that temporary help is all that is needed. Social reform began, however, in the nineteenth century; and since World War II especially, we have increasingly realized that rehabilitation must accompany relief if persons are to escape poverty. The method of dealing with refugees after World War II involved both temporary relief in displaced-persons camps and resettlement and assimilation of such persons into society.

One of the more widely accepted efforts to break the poverty cycle in the 1960's was preschool education for children of the culturally disadvantaged, to enable such children to be more nearly on an equal footing with others when they began school. Job retraining, day care for children of working mothers, tutoring for elementary and high school students— these and many other kinds of aid have been established in an attempt to give the victims of poverty a chance to assume responsibility for themselves.

The problem of poverty in the United States alone is a staggering one; the affluent American can hardly begin to conceive the extent and effects of it on a world-wide scale. For example, it is possible that in some countries, such as India, even the national government can do little to withstand the devastating effects of recurring famine. The refugee problem in the Middle East requires the assistance of the other nations of the world. The resources of the affluent nations are needed to help solve the problem of world poverty. These resources are not just money and food to meet immediate needs; they are also, and in the long run supremely, the technological and economic knowledge and skills for providing measures that will lead to the elimination of poverty-producing conditions.

*The Church and Poverty.* What is the role of the contemporary church in dealing with poverty? The church is very much involved in the relief of suffering through the national Church World Service as well as denominational groups and through the World Council of Churches' Division of Inter-church Aid, Refugee and World Service. The latter group dispenses money and supplies provided by churches of many nations, and has participated in, among other things, the complete rebuilding of villages destroyed by earthquakes or other calamities.[7]

The support by the organized church and by individual Christians of voluntary nonchurch service agencies is likewise to be commended, the support consisting of both money and services. The secularization of social work may be interpreted as the work of God in extending his concern to a larger arena. The call of the Christian is to take seriously the possibility of fulfilling his vocation through working full time in private and public welfare agencies as well as in the institutional church.

The church and the individual Christian also are called to support government efforts both to relieve and to eliminate poverty. All efforts of this kind must be examined, questioned, and modified, of course, for greater efficiency and more adequate fulfillment of their task. The command to love one's neighbor cannot be carried out in a complex and broadly interrelated world through simple charity and individual rehabilitation. That call now involves the Christian in a serious selection of the most adequate means available in dealing with the extensive poverty of the world.

Whether poverty can ever finally be eliminated is a moot question. The issue immediately before us, however, is whether substantial steps can be taken toward its alleviation. It may be given to our period of history—if not this century, then perhaps the next—to make serious inroads into one of the shameful recurring problems of history. In any case, the technological advances of modern man—which are making possible increased food production, the desalination of water, and

[7] For examples of the amount and type of work done by the Division of Inter-Church Aid, Refugee and World Service, see its *Newsletter*, published monthly at 150 Route de Ferney, 1211 Geneva 20, Switzerland.

a controlled population—provide the possibility of a real breakthrough.

## ETHNIC DIVISIONS

A fourth recurring problem in history is the prejudice, the discrimination, and the inhuman treatment of entire groups of human beings. The particular manifestation of this problem in our time is race prejudice, which, though found in most areas of the world, is particularly obvious in South Africa and the United States, between blacks and whites.

*The Nature of Prejudice.* Gordon Allport, in *The Nature of Prejudice,* makes clear that there is no one explanation of the origins of the bitterness between ethnic groups. Often some threat to the security of the majority or in-power group is involved. If one primitive tribe begins to threaten the territorial integrity of another, conflict is likely to arise and prejudice may ensue. Strong ideological positions may lead to prejudice, as when Christians view Jews as Christ-killers. Physical differences between two groups as to color of skin, shape of nose, or kind of hair either may cause prejudice or help keep it alive. The development of stereotypes concerning a feared group may lead to divisions long after the original cause of fear has been removed. Such stereotypes are passed on from one generation to another, for it is clear that children are not born with specific prejudices.

Although children are not born with prejudice, they are born with the capacity for assimilating preformed judgments about persons and groups of people. Whatever the causes of specific ethnic animosities, the self-centeredness of the individual is the primary condition underlying them. The particular objects of prejudice vary; the human condition remains the same. In dealing with the deep feelings accompanying ethnic divisions, therefore, we are not concerned with a problem capable of easy solution. Rather, we are dealing with something deep seated and in need of radical resolution.

*Dealing with Prejudice.* From the Christian perspective, the race problem must be dealt with on two levels—on the level of justice and on that of love. It is probably true, as some theologians insist, that we cannot have justice without love: that is, justice disappears where there is only the cool calculation "of giving everyone his due." Whether this be true or not, the converse side of the situation can readily be affirmed— that sweet sentiments of love are meaningless without the sterner demands for and implementation of justice in the world.

It would be inaccurate to conclude that the church's exhortations to love and brotherhood have had no effect on its members, but it is obvious that such sentiments have not been enough to overcome the racial strife in such nations as the United States and South Africa. Justice, or the demand that right be done, is also necessary. "The voice of justice," writes Haselden, "is the voice of protest, dissent, condemnation. It is the prophetic voice; it uncovers and reveals the corruptions of injustice; it irritates, embarrasses, and denounces the unjust; it lays the ugliness of what is over against the beauty of what should and can be. . . . The voice of justice is a harsh voice, jarring even insensitive nerves." [8]

An important step in the fulfillment of justice in the United States has been the passage of laws guaranteeing all citizens the rights promised them under the Constitution (civil rights legislation). The second step—enforcement of these laws— has not always been taken as soon as the law was passed. Those who have opposed such laws have done so for various reasons, one reason being that it is not possible to legislate personal relationships. Yet in case after case, from the desegregation of buses to equal opportunity in employment, it has been shown that legislation can provide the basis for at least some degree of justice.

The Texas Poll, under the direction of Mr. Joe Belden, found a substantial increase in the toleration of Negro equality by whites in Texas between 1963 and 1968. For example, the percentage of those who accepted desegregation of trains and buses rose from 49 per cent in 1963 to 74 per cent

[8] From *The Racial Problem in Christian Perspective,* by Kyle Haselden (New York: Harper & Brothers, 1959) , p. 107.

in 1968. Approval of the desegregation of eating facilities rose from 40 per cent in 1963 to 70 per cent in 1968 and of sending children to the same schools, from 41 per cent in 1963 to 67 per cent in 1968. Working alongside Negroes rose from 56 per cent in 1963 to 79 per cent in 1968.[9] These statistics indicate that while legalizing a given action may not be enough, law can create conditions under which love can operate more fully: desegregation, a legal matter, can be the prelude to integration, a personal decision.

Whatever may have been accomplished in racial justice, however, there is much to be done beyond justice. A desegregated public high school may still be a place where Afro-American students are not made to feel at home. The organized church bears a great responsibility for helping youth see their responsibility for going beyond mere justice in ethnic matters. In one southern church-related university, the first Negro athlete received a limited number of threatening letters, but the student body and the fans rallied behind him in such a manner that he could hardly have felt other than an integral part of the university community.

The organized church, still one of the most segregated institutions of society, must do more than practice open membership—though it must first do this. It must also seek means whereby the minority group—white, black, some other—truly becomes part of the *koinonia* of those who are one in Jesus Christ.

Beyond the extension of justice and the cultivation of love for minority ethnic groups, Christians are called to work for reconciliation between those groups and individuals whose prejudices are not overcome by the doing of justice. This will be an especially acute problem in the deep South in the years ahead, and it may be scarcely less a problem in other parts of the United States. Beyond justice, a change in persons is required. The Christian knows that he cannot expect too much of the man who has not responded actively to the grace of God, that love of the brother is founded on unsure grounds unless it is related to love of God, and that even the person who has

---

[9] From *The Dallas Morning News*, March 17, 1968, p. 6A.

responded to God is far from perfect in regard to his human relationships.

At the time of history in which this chapter is being completed, we must ask another question for which, quite frankly, I have no answer: Have we in the United States been so long in working out the implications of justice that the black man can no longer see integration as a good? The position that integration is not desirable is maintained by many advocates of "'black power." Although the number in the hard core of this group may not be large, their voices have been heard increasingly since the mid-sixties. These persons often are identified as the advocates of violence and riots. Not all of those who have decided that the true destiny of the black man lies in a black, not an integrated, society advocate violence, however. An increasing emphasis on pride in being black is surely a gain of this general mood. What the repercussions of this larger movement are on relationships between the black and white groups remains to be seen.

The emergence of this dimension in the race problem suggests that there is no one continuing expression of the problems of history. The problems have forms peculiar to our day, but they have had other forms in the past and will have still others in the future. Although historical perspective on such problems is essential, this generation must work to understand their contemporary expression and to bring the necessary skills to bear on the problems of its own time.

## POLITICAL FREEDOM

Political freedom is difficult to define, because many divergent understandings of it obtain. Perhaps the simplest, though relative, definition is that carried in *Webster's Third New International Dictionary of the English Language:* "the ability or capacity to act without undue hindrance or restraint." The implication of this definition—an implication that is quite justified—is that freedom can never exist completely unrestrained, since one man's freedom always restrains another's. The existence of civil law, the competitive nature of business, the contiguousness of persons, all presuppose some degree of hindrance by one person to another's freedom.

It is also difficult to write the *history* of freedom. Was the concept of freedom born among the Hebrews? the Greeks? both? or neither? Perhaps with both, for the Greeks made much of the free citizen, however few in number such persons were. The Hebrew concept of freedom, like its understanding of the nature of man, was theological, and stemmed from man's knowledge of himself as related to the one God in a covenant relationship.

Some *experience* of freedom has often existed even where a people had no conceptual understanding of it. It is difficult to imagine any tribe of people in which every act was completely regulated. In fact, man's personal freedom (apart from his freedom as a political being, or member of organized society) provided some minimal understanding of freedom, as it does in the totalitarian societies today. Generally, however, political and social freedom, or liberty, on any widespread basis is a fairly modern development, dating from the Magna Carta in 1215.

Although freedom in the United States and other Western countries is undergoing continued and serious threats from both the extreme left and the extreme right, it is, at the same time, being sought by races and people that have previously enjoyed relatively few basic human rights. The black man in the United States, the former African colonies, the new nations of Southeast Asia—these are only a few of the groups that are demanding, and to some extent securing, the benefits of freedom. Because many of the new nations are not prepared for freedom, the road ahead for them will not be easy. There is always the danger that they will succumb to some new tyranny —to communism or some other form of dictatorship. One can never afford to be so naïve as to conclude that freedom, once gained, is therefore secure.

Threats to freedom emerge from new and unexpected sources. In the 1930's and 1940's, it was from the extreme left— the actual Communists and those who sympathized with them. In the 1950's and 1960's, it was from the radical right, whose original purpose was partly to hunt out and expose the members of the political left. There is, as various commentators have pointed out, an amazing similarity in the two groups, especially in their tactics. Neither has shown much respect for freedom, especially the freedom of those who disagree. Typical is the John Birch Society, with a monolithic structure for its own organization and a rejection of political conservatives as well as liberals outside that organization.[10]

The freedom the radical movements threaten is primarily political, and it is that kind of freedom with which we are especially concerned here. Forces are also at work to destroy other kinds of freedom, which are just as important. The freedom to be an individual, unfettered by the excessive demands of society, is threatened by a mass society, by the demands of the organization for which one works, by mass communication, and by the trend toward the standardizing of procedures for living. The existence of big business, big labor, and big government as well as mass communication leaves fewer and fewer opportunities for the individual to be, in the words of David Riesman, an inner-directed person.

Part of the trend away from freedom is the unwillingness of individuals to assume responsibility for their lives. Yet freedom and responsibility, on all levels of life—from the most highly personal matter to the most involved political issue—are inextricably related. We cannot have one without the other. Whether or not freedom can continue to survive in the kind of mass society to which we seem to be moving will depend on the capacity of those who believe in freedom to respond to the new forms of society. It may be that some trends can be reversed or at least modified. In any case, the remark of John Curran in a 1790 speech on the right of the election of the Lord Mayor of Dublin is crucial: "The condition upon which God hath given liberty to man is eternal vigilance."

The Christian man, because of his commitment to the One who calls him to responsibility, is committed to the pursuit and maintenance of freedom in the social and political realms. The task of encouraging man to be free is a never-ending one.

[10] See "The John Birch Society: 'Radical Right' and 'Extreme Left' in the Political Context of Post World War II," by Alan F. Westin, in *The Radical Right*, ed. Daniel Bell (Garden City, N.Y.: Anchor Books, 1963), especially pp. 201 ff.

As we saw in a previous chapter, freedom is not automatically accepted; it must be taught and engendered in the young. Man wants too often to escape from freedom; yet without freedom and its accompanying responsibility, there is no adequate Christian life.

## CONCLUSION

In the early years of the twentieth century, there were those both inside and outside the church who genuinely felt that the problems of history would eventually be solved. We are much less sure today of the possibilities for final solutions. Even in a matter such as poverty, in which technological advances play a significant role and provide the physical possibility of feeding the world, we cannot be sure that we will be able to work out problems of distribution, which involve human as well as technical matters.

The question for the Christian is not whether the basic problems of history can be *eliminated,* but rather how they can be *alleviated.* In dealing with these problems, the concern of the Christian is not alone with "holy history" but also with general history. He is a participant in all of history by virtue of his being a live human being. He has, therefore, responsibility toward all aspects of history—a responsibility to work in his own way, however undramatic his role may be, for the improvement of the lot of mankind and of relationships among men.

As one reads history, he becomes increasingly aware that problems do not cease to exist. When one is eliminated, another appears in its place. There *is* a kind of cyclical character to history seen just from the human viewpoint, though there is some resolution as well as recurrence of problems. This is a part of the challenge of life to which man responds if he is to live meaningfully. All of us are makers of history. One way we make it is to work responsibly in the occasions of our daily life. This is our task and our calling.

# Chapter IX

# THE TEACHING
# OF HISTORY

Understanding history is a way of arriving at self-under-standing. By the very process of living, all of us are involved in history, or actually in a number of histories. We are so influenced by these histories, both those in which we partici-pate directly and those which come out of the more distant past, that we cannot understand ourselves without knowing something of their meaning.

The questions that have concerned us thus far are therefore relevant to the lives of all persons; for we have considered the meaning and interpretation of history, its issues and major problems. Some matters are of special interest to those engaged in the teaching of history, however; and this chapter is devoted to questions pertinent to the teaching of history to elementary boys and girls and high school youth.

The teaching of history must be seen against the background of what has been said thus far. Any person who studies, teaches, or writes history, for example, needs to be aware that he views history from a particular perspective—at times even from a distorted perspective. Recently discovered evidence, for example, has necessitated some radical rethinking of our interpretation of the Middle Ages, since even the time at which this period began is in dispute. As the Roman Catholic Church has looked at the Reformation from the vantage point of Vatican II, new perspectives have been opened to Catholic leaders and laymen, including a desire to sing the reformer Martin Luther's "A Mighty Fortress."

The Christian interpreter of history certainly must realize that not all people view history from his point of view. The Christian belief that history is fulfilled outside itself, in the purposes of God, is not universally accepted, for example. Although the Jewish and the Christian interpretations have much in common, they are not identical because of the Christian understanding of Jesus Christ as the "hinge of history" (its crucial point of interpretation). To recognize one's self as belonging to a called community, either Jewish or Christian, means that one views all of life in a particular way. We have examined this basic concept in earlier chapters, and therefore should be prepared to understand the Christian view as one, but not the only, perspective from which history is understood.

Nor is it possible, as some would seek to do, to separate the life of the called community from the world and to have, as it were, two ways of viewing life and history, the Sunday and the weekday. I have tried to stress, as perhaps no other point, the fact that the Christian looks at all of life—society and/ or history—from a particular perspective and does not separate the "religious" from the "secular" in any definitive fashion. By now it should be clear that the Christian does not seek to *impose* his view on other people; rather, he accepts it as the way in which he views life, as other people look at life and history from other perspectives.

Briefly stated, this perspective interprets history as the medium of God's self-disclosure: that is, in both the past and the present, the action of God can be perceived in *those things which happen* in human affairs. God has revealed himself not *only* in Jesus Christ nor even in the Jewish-Christian tradition, but the Christian finds the key to understanding *all* of God's revelation in Christ. In light of this revelation, man is called to work responsibly in obedience to God and in relationship with his fellow men. Man is accountable in history—that is, in human relationships. History, then, is not self-contained or self-fulfilling, but finds its meaning and fulfillment in relation to God, the Ground of its being.

## OTHER PERSPECTIVES

History is understood, written, and taught from other perspectives, as I have repeatedly pointed out. One of the more obvious ones in our time is that of Marxism, or communism. Karl Marx viewed history as self-fulfilling through the dialectical process—that is, by forces operating in the nature of life itself (deterministic), the dictatorship of the proletariat (the present stage of communism), then eventually the withering away of the state, and finally complete equality among men (the millennium) will come about.

The communist view of history is, like that of the Hebrew-Christian tradition, linear; for the processes of history are viewed as leading somewhere. Although communism is deterministic in that the process is said to be inevitable, it, like many other forms of determinism, is not fatalistic. Rather, it leads many of its followers to a crusade for the attainment of the classless society. Marxism is historically oriented to the fullest extent.

The clear-cut character of its historical goal makes the theory of Marxism fairly easy to identify. The processes of life are to be so channeled that they will contribute to the realization of the classless society. All reality is interpreted as materialistic (a fact that makes communism a substitute for religion and thus a rival to Christian faith). Thus the most important aspects of history are those pertaining to the realization of the economic aims of mankind.

It is more difficult to identify other perspectives from which history is taught, partly because their goals are less specific.

For example, what is the goal of history for most Americans? Because of a certain lack of clarity concerning national goals, history and the social studies are often taught from the perspective of good citizenship, with not too much meaning to the idea.

One group in the United States that is fairly clear especially concerning that which it *opposes* is the far right (or radical right). "Americanism" is identified with opposition to governmental control and support of extreme *laissez-faire* capitalism. The adherents of the far right wish to make the public schools a platform for opposition to anything that might be called "liberal" and to propagate a view of life something like that supported by the conservatives of the nineteenth century. In order to secure their goals, many members of the far right would resort to methods similar to those advocated by fascism and communism for controlling society.

At the opposite end of the scale politically are those educational theorists often called the "social reconstructionists." From their perspective, society is viewed as dynamic, moving toward more adequate forms, but in need of radical reform. The school is thought of as an agency of social change; and social studies, including history, are viewed as the curriculum areas in which change can be most readily encouraged.

Perhaps the most common perspective might be termed the sentimental "our country is a good place to live; let's keep it that way" point of view. More conservative than reactionary, the position nevertheless aims more at appreciation than change. Its attitude toward religion is encouragement so long as faith is limited to personal, pietistic forms and avoids social involvement. This view tends to identify religion with "the American way of life" and to describe it as a kind of general belief in God and in morality—what Martin Marty calls "religion in general." The following quotation from a high school textbook in citizenship is illustrative:

> My attitude toward religion can be that of seeking the truth wherever it is to be found and accepting it when I become convinced that it is the truth. In this search for truth, I can constantly try to be fair to those with whom I may not always agree. I can set up as my models

and guides the great teachers of religion and morals and try to practice their teachings. I can keep on even when I make discouraging mistakes.[1]

Still another position includes something of both of the two just considered. The task of the social studies is thought of as both preservation and change, but with the emphasis on the necessity of change. For example, Tiegs and Adams, in a textbook on the teaching of social studies, point to the tremendous changes occurring in our world and the possibilities for both good and evil within them. They then identify what they think to be the objective of the teacher of social studies in the schools:

> Social studies teachers, through their ability to help pupils acquire desirable knowledges, attitudes, and problem-solving skills and to inspire them to dynamic and intelligent participation, will play a significant part in helping our future citizens to control and use these mighty forces for the good of all mankind. In a very real sense, therefore, the form of the future is being cast in the social studies classrooms of the nation.[2]

It is not my purpose here to enter into a discussion of the purposes of public education, especially in regard to the teaching of history and the other social studies. It is only as that purpose is related to or comes into conflict with the nature of Christian faith that we are concerned. In this connection, two questions must be raised. First, where does the teaching of love of country and a healthy patriotism end, and the teaching of a narrow nationalism that tends to become a religion begin? If Herberg and Marty and others are right (and I believe they are), all three of the major American religious groups (Catholic, Protestant, and Jewish) have tended to identify their own

---

[1] From page 292 of *Building Citizenship*, revised by James H. McCrocklin. Copyright © 1961, 1965 by Allyn and Bacon, Inc. Reprinted by permission of Allyn and Bacon, Inc.

[2] From *Teaching the Social Studies: A Guide to Better Citizenship*, by Ernest W. Tiegs and Fay Adams (New York: Ginn and Company, 1959), p. 1.

faith with the American way of life, and have thus tended toward a religion in general that affirms the value of God, motherhood, and country but neglects those distinctly Jewish or Christian beliefs, values, and practices.

The second question that must be asked about any general teaching of moral and religious values is whether these values are identified with the absolute or whether they are seen as approximations, at best, of the absolute. For the Jew and the Christian, the only absolute is God. All human achievements are only incomplete realizations of the highest good. The long sweep of history helps us perceive this fact. What is considered just today may be condemned as unjust in some future generation. All our actions are under the judgment of God, though we must act as best we can under the circumstances and are held accountable for doing so.

Holding in tension an appreciation of both past and present with a recognition of the necessity of change now and in the future is not easy. We are constantly tempted either to absolutize the past or the present or to become cynical about them. Whether or not the public schools can maintain this tension is a question I cannot answer. If the schools cannot, then it becomes even more important that the churches help the young both appreciate the achievements of the past and act for constructive change. The churches can do this as they remember, on the one hand, that God is known in history through his self-revelation and, on the other, that history is dynamic (changing) because it is the arena of God's continued action. As man responds more fully to what God is now doing as well as to what he has done in the past, the changes that are necessary in the realm of values can be effected.

## THE CONTENT OF PUBLIC SCHOOL TEACHING

The *perspective* from which teaching occurs is both more difficult to deal with and more important than the content itself, at least when we are dealing with history. We can without too much trouble identify the major concerns of the public schools in teaching history. We can judge, even though sub-

147

jectively, whether or not organized religion as a phenomenon of culture receives just consideration, as it rightfully should, in history courses. We can also, without, I think, violating the principle of separation of church and state, introduce more elements of teaching *about* religion into the public school curriculum.

Partly because content is easier to deal with than is perspective, content has received most attention in the recent controversy over the secularization of public education. When we conclude, as many have, that the schools have tended to substitute secularism for traditional theistic religion, we are dealing with a more difficult question. Although we cannot avoid this more fundamental question concerning perspective and basic orientation, we need also to look at the way in which religion is treated as a datum of the subject matter of history.

It is, first, necessary to give some indication of how the social studies are organized. The term *social studies* refers to various aspects of human relationships. They "comprise an area of the curriculum which is concerned primarily with the nature, manifestations, and development of various types of human relations." [3] They include such separate subject areas as history, geography, civics, sociology, and the like. Although our chief concern is history, we must see it, especially in the elementary grades, as only one aspect of the larger area of the social studies.

Four ways of organizing the traditional subjects comprising the social studies are possible, according to Tiegs and Adams (pages 52 ff.) . First, they may be organized as separate subjects, with history, for example, being one of the designated subjects. Second, they may be correlated, though maintained as separate subjects. Third, they may be fused, so that subject matter from several different fields is included in the same course of study. History, geography, social structures, economics, and the like may be included in the same text, with the subject being called social studies, history, or something else. The fourth is the integrated curriculum, in which the

[3] *Ibid.,* p. 49.

focus of organization is on "the achievement of knowledges, insights, understandings, attitudes, appreciations, and skills related to the development of desirable human relationships." [4] In other words, the organizing principle is really not subject matter, but relationships; subject matter is used as a means of encouraging better relationships.

Following these four types, a survey was made in the early 1950's of how social studies courses are organized across the nation. It was found that, in city schools, 58 per cent of the courses were integrated at the level of grade one; 33 per cent were fused; 6 per cent were correlated; and 3 per cent were separate. By grade six, the percentages had changed so that 34 per cent were integrated, 24 per cent fused, 28 per cent correlated, and 13 per cent separate. In grade seven, the integrated, fused, and correlated courses were still more common than separated subjects; but in grade eight, separate subjects were more common than were those with various degrees of relatedness.[5]

Surveys have also been made of the subject matter most common at the various grade levels. Table I gives the results of one such survey made by Edwin R. Carr for The Center for Applied Research in Education, with the most common subject matter for each grade listed first.[6]

## TABLE I

Most Common Subject Matters in Social Studies Programs

| Grade | Subject |
|---|---|
| 1 | Life at home and at school; pets; holidays; farm life |
| 2 | Community helpers and workers; transportation; communication |

[4] *Ibid.*, pp. 54-55.

[5] From *Organization and Content of the Social Studies Curriculum*, by Frank M. Hodgson (Unpublished Ed.D. dissertation, University of Southern California, 1953) ; cited in *Teaching the Social Studies: A Guide to Better Citizenship*, pp. 54-55.

[6] From *The Social Studies*, by Edwin R. Carr (New York: The Center for Applied Research in Education, Inc., 1965), p. 7. Used by permission. A somewhat different listing is found in Tiegs and Adams, pp. 56-58.

3 Expanding community; food, clothing, shelter; other communities
4 Living in other lands (type geographic regions); state history; state geography
5 United States history and geography; Latin America; Canada; Western Hemisphere
6 Geography of Western Hemisphere; geography of Eastern Hemisphere; Old World backgrounds of the history of the United States
7 Geography of Eastern Hemisphere; world geography; United States History
8 United States History; geography; state history; civics
9 Civics; vocations; world history; world geography
10 World history; world geography; modern history
11 United States history; world history; problems of democracy; civics
12 Problems of democracy; government; economics, sociology; United States history

Although the list of subjects by grades in Tiegs and Adams is not identical with the one presented in Table I, there are a great many parallels between the two lists. Together the two lists indicate that agreement is fairly high concerning what should be covered in the various grades. Since this agreement is only in part, however, and since in no instance is there only one subject listed for a grade, any church group wishing to relate its teaching to what is happening in the public schools must be informed about the approach and content of the particular school or schools its children and youth attend.

## THE RELIGIOUS CONTENT OF TEXTBOOKS

Although the best teachers usually do not slavishly follow textbooks, many others do, and all are influenced by them. While each teacher brings his or her particular perspective to the teaching of any subject, the text is usually the most influential outside force on his teaching. Probably in most instances the text is crucial to the manner in which the teacher will develop a unit; it is also influential in the ideas the teacher presents. It is therefore significant in our inquiries into the approach to social studies in our schools that we take some note of the religious content of texts or of the omission of it and, insofar as we can, of the perspective from which these texts are written.

A limited number of surveys have been made of public school textbooks and the extent to which they include religion as part of their subject matter. One such study, made by the American Council on Education in 1948, concerned the larger field of intergroup relations. Two conclusions of this study are pertinent. They have been summarized by Judah J. Harris for the Anti-Defamation League of B'nai B'rith as follows:

> 1. Under the heading "Treatment of Religious Groups," the report concluded that textbooks assumed the desirability of religious groupings in society while pointing out that one of the causes of intergroup friction was misunderstanding caused by religious differences. The Inquisition period was evaluated by many texts outside of its historical context, and the evangelical aspects of Protestantism were sometimes caricatured. The study maintained that "too little appears in the texts on the exact nature of religious groups (either their differences or their likenesses) or on the common concern of church groups with ethical or humanitarian developments."

> 2. Under the heading "Treatment of Jews," the study observed that three-fourths of the space allotted to Jews in world history texts dealt with events before 70 c.e. The assumption seemed to be that Judaism and Jewish culture had changed little since then. Reference to Jews after that date was usually in connection with persecution. There was little about constructive contributions of the group or about their relations with other groups.[7]

[7] From *The Treatment of Religion in Elementary Social Studies Textbooks*, by Judah J. Harris (New York: Anti-Defamation League of B'nai B'rith, 315 Lexington Avenue, New York, N.Y. 10016, 1963), p. 3. Reprinted with permission of the Anti-Defamation League of B'nai B'rith. Based on *Intergroup Relations in Teaching Materials: A Survey and Appraisal* (American Council on Education, 1948).

A second survey, in the form of an unpublished doctoral dissertation, was made in 1950 by Harold Pflug and was limited to textbooks used in Missouri. He sampled 113 texts in geography, reading, science, social science (social studies), and literature from grades one through twelve. His conclusions were:

> 1. The number and volume of theistic religious references increases with advancing school grades. . . .
> 2. The concepts used are inadequately defined, described, and interpreted. . . .
> 3. The references deal largely with the outward expressions of religion, only rarely with religion as an inner experience.
> 4. It is possible to deal objectively and informatively with controversial matters.
> 5. The closer we get to textbook descriptions of present-day life and literature, the fewer theistic religious references there are. . . . Thus an alert student may feel that the textbook dealing with today's problems no longer cites religion as a molding force in society.[8]

Another study, sponsored by the Danforth Foundation and reported in 1956, concerned the treatment of religion in North Carolina high schools. Confining his study to thirty-four English and social science texts for all grades, John B. Bennett found very little notice of religion in these books. He concluded that if any religious orientation were to be expected of the schools in North Carolina, it would have to come from the individual teacher or the extracurricular program of the schools.

A more extensive survey of texts was made in 1962 by Judah J. Harris under the auspices of the Anti-Defamation League of B'nai B'rith, in his *The Treatment of Religion in Elementary Social Studies Textbooks*. It involved 120 social studies texts in the elementary grades, the majority having been published in the 1950's. Mr. Harris' conclusions are

[8] From *Theistic Religion in Missouri Public School Textbooks*, by Harold A. Pflug (Unpublished dissertation, Yale University, 1950), p. 330. Quoted in *ibid.*, pp. 1-2.

somewhat different from those of the other three, since he found considerable stress on the importance of religion as a motivating force in the past history of mankind. He agrees, however, that, while the textbooks pay considerable attention to the place of religion in the past, they say little about its part in contemporary life. One may conclude that the over-all impression such books give is that religion is no longer a significant force in society.

Mr. Harris, writing from a Jewish perspective, also concludes that religion is not treated with much objectivity in many of the texts. He finds the most obvious examples of anti-Catholic bias in the handling of the Reformation. "The facts concerning Jewish history and Judaism, too, are presented in a manner that lacks objectivity and completeness," he goes on to say. "The delicate subject of the Crucifixion is often dealt with imprudently, in a fashion that tends to stimulate prejudice." [9]

On the basis of his study, Harris also concluded that Christianity is treated in some of the books as being synonymous with everything that is good. By implication, Harris believes, everything not Christian may be concluded as bad.

Perhaps the most common criticism of the surveys (one borne out by the survey I made, which will be reported shortly) is that religion in contemporary life is given short shrift. "The texts," Harris writes, "portray present-day religion as no longer being a potent molding force in our society." Elementary public school social studies textbooks tend to present the role of religion in the past in an adequate fashion "but to give a sketchy, incomplete description of the part played by present-day religion in contemporary culture. . . ." The three manifestations of contemporary Christianity most often mentioned are church attendance, worship, and welfare work. Further, "practically all of the information conveyed about the Jews relates to events occurring over 2,000 years ago. Virtually nothing is said about Jewish life in America today." [10]

[9] Harris, *op. cit.*, p. 51.
[10] *Ibid.*, pp. 52-53.

I have examined a limited number (twenty-four) of social studies (primarily history) texts for grades one through twelve. All but three of the texts were published in 1960 or later, two of the others being editions of one book, published in 1956 and 1958. There may or may not be any significance in the later publication dates, though it is true that the Supreme Court decision of 1962 against a stated prayer's being used in the New York schools was a culmination of previous decisions and of a growing sentiment for the exclusion of religious exercises from public education.

By way of background, it should be said that these texts are less concerned with the political side of life (rulers, presidents, wars, and the like) than books once were and that, on the other hand, they are more interested in daily life and other socio-cultural matters. There is considerable emphasis on "middle class virtues"—honesty, love of country, decency, and the like. There is much good material on such issues as international relations and other problems. There is no evidence of the influence of the extreme right in these particular books.

On the other hand, there is not a great deal of treatment of religion except in the texts dealing with non-American history—that is, in world history, including the history of Europe. Especially in the lower grades is there little mention of religion. There is no consistency in the way religion is dealt with, especially in American life. For some reason, the Quakers seem to have come off rather better than other religious groups. In one book of American biography, William Penn is the only American leader included who has much to do with religion.[11] In some of the world history books, the non-Christian and non-Jewish religions are treated more adequately than any of the major American religious groups. In one, for example, five pages are devoted to the religions of the Far East and three to Islam; but no comparable section can be found having to do with Christianity or Judaism.[12] In another, there are

[11] See *Great Names in American History*, by Harold H. Eibling, Fred M. King, and James Harlow (River Forest, Ill.: Laidlaw Brothers, Publishers, 1965).

[12] See *Exploring a Changing World*, by Melvin Schwartz and John O'Connor (New York: Globe Book Company, 1966). See also *The World*

numerous references to Christianity, so that, if these references were to be put together, that faith would come off rather well. Interestingly, however, Islam receives more than three pages of consecutive material and Buddhism a similar amount, but Hebrew religion gets about one-half page, concerned only with the early Hebrew period.[13]

It is worth noting, also, that the later edition of one text, in discussing the beginnings of Hebrew religion, makes a curious change. The first edition begins a section on early Hebrew religion in this manner: "Most important of all the little groups of people [in the Middle East] were the Hebrews." [14] The later edition, published only two years later, begins an almost identical section in this fashion: "The Bible tells us how the Hebrews. . . ." [15]

There is a surprisingly inadequate treatment of religion as a factor in the settling and progress of early America. Some reference usually is made to the religious motivation of the Puritans and the Pilgrims, and writers seem to find it difficult to discuss Roger Williams and William Penn without considering the religious factors in their contributions to American life. Religion on the frontier receives but little treatment in spite of the rather significant influence of Protestantism on both frontier life and culture. As brief as is the quotation that follows, it is the most adequate found in the texts examined. It is interesting to note, also, the extent to which religion becomes conflated with Americanism (or religion in general).

> Nearly all of the frontier villages had a church. Few of the churches, however, could afford a full-time

*Today: Its Patterns and Cultures,* by Clyde F. Kohn and Dorothy Weitz Drummond (New York: Webster Division, McGraw-Hill Book Company, 1963).

[13] See *Our Widening World: A History of the World's Peoples,* by Ethel E. Ewing (Chicago: Rand McNally & Company, 1961).

[14] From *Man's Story: World History in Its Geographic Setting,* by T. Walter Wallbank (Chicago: Scott, Foresman and Company, 1956). p. 54.

[15] From *Living World History,* by T. Walter Wallbank and Arnold Fletcher (later edition of *Man's Story: World History in Its Geographic Setting;* Chicago: Scott, Foresman and Company, 1958), p. 51.

preacher. One preacher rode around to many small towns. He visited each town once or twice a year. The circle of towns he visited was called a circuit. For this reason the preacher was called a *circuit rider*.

Even when the people could not attend church, they tried to do right. Their code of living was: help one another; harm no one; and trust in God. This code of living is part of our rich heritage. It is a heritage of which we can be proud. It is a heritage we must all try to live by. Then our nation will remain great and strong! [16]

In the same book, a diary of life in the Colonies (pages 176-181) excludes Sunday altogether!

There are exceptions to the lack of treatment of religion in American life, however. *Our Free Nation,* an eighth-grade text, has considerably more material than most of the others; and this includes the modern period. Even the ecumenical movement receives notice, and the National Council of Churches is named. It should be noted, however, that the orientation is primarily toward Protestant Christianity.

We may conclude on the basis of these four surveys, then, that organized religion receives fairly adequate treatment in relation to the non-Christian lands and even in regard to Europe. The treatment of religion in Europe is often lacking in objectivity, though there appears an effort to be fair in recent writing. Jewish religion and culture, however, receive little attention, especially in their modern manifestations. Harris is probably right in his conclusion that textbooks still tend to be Protestant oriented.

Generally the American religious heritage is inadequately presented in social studies textbooks. Even the tradition of religious freedom and the separation of church and state is not discussed with any adequacy. There is but little recognition of the contributions of Protestant Christianity to American life in many of the texts, and virtually none regarding

[16] From *America's Story,* by Vanza Devereaux [with Frank L. Williams, Martin Ridge, and Chester D. Babcock] (San Francisco: Harr Wagner Publishing Co., 1962), p. 242. Used by permission of Field Educational Publications, Inc.

Roman Catholicism and Judaism. The greatest weakness, as indicated by most of those who have surveyed textbooks, is in regard to modern life. Apparently the writers either do not see the significance of organized religion, or else they are afraid to deal with it. According to most of the texts, American life today could just as well be completely bereft of organized religion.

It is not easy to draw conclusions concerning the perspective of social studies texts, though the general approach seems to be a cautious Americanism. No evidence was found of the unhealthy nationalism of the extreme right. Indeed, it is difficult to object to any one thing the texts contain. It is, rather, what they do *not* say that must be called to question. For, as we have already seen, the demonic character of Americanism is that it may become a substitute for religion. It is centered in nationalistic goals and ideas, while religion is centered in God, who is both the sustainer and the judge of all life, including that of the United States. Whether or not this latter perspective could ever be incorporated into a text for general use is a question which I do not presume to answer. It is noted here only because of its relevance for the church's concern not only for the subject matter included in the teaching of history but also for the perspective from which history is taught. In the final analysis, the latter is of more importance; yet it seems almost impossible to deal with in a pluralistic school system.

## WHAT ARE THE ISSUES?

Although our primary concern in this book is not with the relation of religion to public education, we cannot avoid giving that problem some consideration. Our survey of the way in which organized religion is treated in history books and in other social studies texts used in the public schools has been primarily to pose the problem of how the church is to deal with the lack of a Christian perspective in the teaching of history and with the failure of public school texts even to treat adequately organized religion as a cultural fact. It seems appropriate, however, that we look briefly at the issues involved in the relation of religion to public education. Three merit our attention.

The first is this: Is religious teaching in the public schools constitutional? Recent Supreme Court decisions have with few exceptions been in the direction of removing religion from the public schools. The decision causing the greatest excitement was the Regent's Prayer Case, concerning the use of a prescribed prayer in the schools of New York state. The court ruled that the practice was unconstitutional. Of equal importance was the case in 1963 concerning the Pennsylvania requirement that teachers read at least ten verses from the Bible without comment each day. This provision was also declared unconstitutional under the "Establishment Clause" of the First Amendment to the Constitution.

Perhaps, however, the most significant part of the Opinion for the Court, written by Mr. Justice Clark, is a reference to the way in which religion *may* be considered in public schools. After asserting that the Court's decision does not, in the opinion of the Court, establish a "religion of secularism" for the schools, Justice Clark goes on to say:

> In addition, it might well be said that one's education is not complete without a study of comparative religion or the history of religion and its relationship to the advancement of civilization. It certainly may be said that the Bible is worthy of study for its literary and historic qualities. Nothing we have said here indicates that such study of the Bible or of religion, when presented objectively, as part of a secular program of education, may not be effected consistent with the First Amendment.[17]

It has been rightly concluded, I believe, that the Supreme Court through this statement has not only made explicit its *approval* of teaching *about* religion as a part of public education; it has gone a step further and has *encouraged* such teaching. It would appear that it is permissible not only to present subject matter relative to religion as a part of culture, but also that various perspectives on history may be discussed so long

[17] Quoted from *Cornerstones of Religious Freedom in America,* ed. Joseph L. Blau, p. 289.

as a serious attempt is made to be fair to all of them and no one is presented as the only acceptable one.

The second issue follows closely from the first: Is it *possible* to teach objectively, especially when the subject is religion? The answer suggested in previous sections of this book would appear to be in the negative. Much has been said concerning the fact that history is inevitably presented from some perspective, either implicit or explicit. We cannot repeat the discussion of this issue, which was considered at some length in Chapter II. In summary, the conclusion was that, while the historian cannot avoid his perspective completely, he can be fair in his dealing both with facts and with differing points of view. The responsible historian—as writer, teacher, or other person concerned with the past—uses the best methods of historical research and study he can muster, recognizes his biases, and seeks to be fair knowing that he cannot be completely objective.

The ability to deal with any controversial subject must be cultivated, whether that subject be the Protestant Reformation or the present differences between adherents of liberal and conservative political ideologies. Schools often fear controversy and understandably (though not justifiably) avoid subjects on which strong feelings exist, one of these subjects being religion. Much of the reason for avoiding controversy could be eliminated if teachers were adequately prepared to deal fairly and justly with subject matter on which there are differences of opinion.

One important step in acquiring the ability to deal with controversy is to recognize one's own biases. Perhaps teachers ought to be advised in some instances to make their biases explicit. A Roman Catholic teacher might introduce a study of the Protestant Reformation with a recognition that he cannot fully extricate himself (nor should he be required to do so) from his religious heritage. As a further step, textbooks can be prepared by representatives of various points of view— by persons acting either as writers or consultants—to help teachers deal with specific historical aspects of religion (such as the Spanish Inquisition). Occasionally, it may be appropriate to have clergymen or laymen outside the school personally present differing perspectives on the same data of history, especially to high school students. The result of this kind of method would, among other things, help students become aware that history is not written with complete objectivity.

In answer to the question, Can history be taught objectively? we must give a qualified "no." Such teaching would probably be very dull, even if it could be done. Rather, we are suggesting two things: first, the teacher can seek to be honest and fair in dealing with all historical and contemporary subject matter. Second, he can be encouraged to examine his presuppositions and to make them clear to his students. One of the functions of the church might be to help teachers recognize the implicit assumptions both in textbooks and in their own teaching.

The third question is this: What are the possible ways of dealing with religion in public school courses? Since this is part of the subject to be considered in Chapter X, only the question is raised here. Chapter X also will give special attention to what the church can do to supplement the teaching of history by the public schools.

## SOCIAL STUDIES TEXTBOOKS CONSULTED

*Grade 1.*

Samford, Clarence, Edith McCall, and Ruth Gue. *You and the Neighborhood.* Chicago: Benefic Press, 1965. Contains an excellent chapter on churches.

Wann, Kenneth D., and Emma D. Sheehy. *Learning About Our Families,* "Living in Our Times" series. Boston: Allyn and Bacon, Inc., 1962.

*Grade 2.*

Hanna, Paul R., and Genevieve Anderson Hoyt (with William S. Gray). *In the Neighborhood.* Chicago: Scott, Foresman and Company, 1958.

Wann, Kenneth D., Frances C. Wann, and Emma D. Sheehy. *Learning About Our Neighbors.,* "Living in Our Times" series. Boston: Allyn and Bacon, Inc., 1962.

## Grade 3.

Hunnicutt, C. W., and Jean D. Grambs. *Your Community and Mine.* Syracuse: The L. W. Singer Company (A Division of Random House, Inc.), 1966.

Sorensen, Clarence W., *Ways of Our Land.* Morristown, N.J.: Silver Burdett Company, 1965.

Thomas, Eleanor (with Ernest W. Tiegs and Fay Adams). *Your Town and Mine.* Boston: Ginn and Company, 1960.

## Grade 4.

Eibling, Harold H., Fred M. King, and James Harlow. *World Background for American History.* "Laidlaw History" series. River Forest, Ill.: Laidlaw Brothers, Publishers (A Division of Doubleday & Co., Inc.), 1965. Contains considerable material on religion.

Hanna, Paul R., Clyde F. Kohn, and Robert A. Lively. *In All Our States.* Chicago: Scott, Foresman and Company, 1961.

## Grade 5.

Burnette, O. Lawrence, Jr., and Lettie Lee Ralph. *Life in America: Past and Present.* New York: Harper & Row, 1964, 1965.

Clark, Thomas D., Ray Compton, and Amber Wilson. *America's Frontier.* Chicago: Lyons and Carnahan, 1958, 1962.

Eibling, Harold H., Fred M. King, and James Harlow. *Great Names in American History.* River Forest, Ill.: Laidlaw Brothers, Publishers, 1965.

## Grade 6.

Hanna, Paul R., Clyde F. Kohn, and Robert A. Lively. *Beyond the Americas.* Chicago: Scott, Foresman and Company, 1964.

## Grades 7 through 9.

Schwartz, Melvin, and John O'Connor. *Exploring a Changing World: A Geography of World Regions and Their Cultures.* New York: Globe Book Company, 1966.

## Grade 8.

Devereaux, Vanza (with Frank L. Williams, Martin Ridge, and Chester D. Babcock). *America's Story.* San Francisco: Field Educational Publications., 1962.

Eibling, Harold H., Fred M. King, and James Harlow (with Rubert J. Rayback). *History of Our United States.* River Forest, Ill.: Laidlaw Brothers, Publishers, 1964.

McGuire, Edna, and Thomas B. Portwood. *Our Free Nation.* New

York: The Macmillan Company, 1961. Contains a rather good treatment of religion, but primarily Protestant oriented.

Schwartz, Melvin, and John O'Connor. *Exploring American History.* New York: Globe Book Company, 1963.

### Grade 9.

Boak, Arthur E. R., Preston W. Slosson, Howard R. Anderson, and Hall Bartlett. *The History of Our World.* Boston: Houghton Mifflin Company, 1961.

Ewing, Ethel E. *Our Widening World: A History of the World's Peoples.* Chicago: Rand McNally & Company, 1961.

### Grades 10 through 12.

Hughes, Ray Osgood; rev. by James H. McCrocklin. *Building Citizenship.* Boston: Allyn and Bacon, Inc., rev. ed., 1965.

Kohn, Clyde F., and Dorothy Weitz Drummond. *The World Today: Its Patterns and Cultures.* New York: Webster Division, McGraw Hill Book Company, 1963.

Wallbank, T. Walter. *Man's Story: World History in Its Geographic Setting.* Chicago: Scott, Foresman and Company, 1956.

Wallbank, T. Walter, and Arnold Fletcher. *Living World History* (a revision of *Man's Story*). Chicago: Scott, Foresman and Company, 1958.

# Chapter X

# THE CHURCH AND THE TEACHING OF HISTORY

In our discussion thus far, we have moved from general questions concerning the value of reading and studying history to more specific ones regarding the teaching of that subject in the public schools. Our interest in public school teaching grows out of a Christian view of history. If, as we have tried to show, Christian faith is related specifically and integrally to history, then the way the subject matter of history is presented to children and youth concerns churchmen.

Concrete questions must be raised, therefore, concerning the church and the teaching of history. How can the organized church act responsibly in relation to the teaching of history when by far the greatest part of that teaching is done in publicly supported schools? Is the only responsibility of the church to see that the history of the church is taught somewhere? Or is the job of the church to seek means of teaching all history from the Christian perspective? Does the church seek to find ways of encouraging public schools to teach the facts of religious history and the religious perspective? Or does the church supplement public school teaching by teaching church history and by helping persons view history from a Christian perspective?

The answers to these questions are not easy to come by; nor is there anything like a consensus concerning them. Although it is not our purpose here to present a complete analysis of the relationship of religion and public education in the United States, some account must be taken of this relationship if we are to deal realistically with what the church can do to implement the concerns of earlier chapters.

## THE PROBLEM

The public schools of the United States are among the few educational systems in the West without some legal or organizational relationship to organized religion. Whereas in the United States the trend has been to remove most religion from public schools, England has taken a somewhat different course. By its Education Act of 1944, England increased, or at least standardized, the required teaching of religion in publicly supported schools (including both state schools and private schools receiving public money). Although increasing dissatisfaction has been expressed concerning the quality of such teaching, religious teaching is still mandatory in all such schools. Most European countries outside the communist orbit have similar provisions.

Several factors govern the situation regarding the teaching of religion in the United States. One of these is the principle of the separation of church and state established by the First Amendment to the Constitution. There is no agreement concerning how rigid the Founding Fathers intended this separation to be, and many persons today feel that the principle has been interpreted far too strictly.

Perhaps more influential in the development of public schools not related to organized religion has been the religious pluralism of the United States. School officials began early in the nineteenth century to face the problem of the kind of religious instruction to be provided for an increasingly heterogeneous population. William Kailer Dunn, a Roman Catholic, concludes that pluralism, not antagonism toward religion, was the chief cause for the decline of religious education in public schools between 1776 and 1861.[1]

The inability to agree over the aspects of religion appropriate to public education continues to be a factor in secularization. More recently the chief objections have been raised by parents who feel that their children are obliged to participate in some form of religious exercise or teaching to which they do not subscribe. When the schools have indicated that these children might be excused from such exercises, parents have raised questions concerning the emotional effects on children not taking part in those acts engaged in by the majority.

Not unimportant in the objection to religious exercises in public schools, however, has been the feeling on the part of churchmen that instruction in faith or devotions—even indirectly as in the use of a prayer—is not the job of the public schools.

The process of secularization[2]—continuing since early in the nineteenth century—has been accelerated since World War II. Pressure has been brought to bear on the schools and subsequently in the courts to remove various forms of religious expression from the schools. The process has resulted in a series of decisions, beginning in 1948, by the United States Supreme Court.

The earliest of these postwar decisions related to "released time," a plan in operation for more than three decades prior to the 1948 decision. Released time provides for the release

---

[1] See *What Happened to Religious Education?* by William Kailer Dunn (Baltimore: The Johns Hopkins Press, 1958), p. 309.

[2] For a documentation of this process, see *ibid.*; also *The Secularization of American Education*, by Samuel Windsor Brown (Teachers' College, Columbia University Contributions to Education, No. 49; New York: Teachers' College, Columbia University, 1912).

of students by the public schools for one hour each week for religious instruction by the churches. Two plans were in use prior to 1948—instruction which occurred on school property and that which took place elsewhere.

A suit by Mrs. Vashti McCollum of Champaign, Illinois, sought to prevent the schools of that city from carrying on a program of released-time instruction in public school buildings. In 1948 the case was decided by the United States Supreme Court in favor of Mrs. McCollum. As one writer has put it:

> An important new precedent was established in the McCollum decision. The Supreme Court denied that "the purpose of the 'establishment' clause was only to insure protection for the 'free exercise of religion.'" For the first time in American jurisprudence, a plaintiff was allowed to invoke the First Amendment against a practice which aids religion without any infringement of his own rights.[3]

Four years later, in 1952, the Court affirmed a decision by the New York State Court of Appeals that would permit released-time classes conducted on school time but not on school property.[4]

Two other decisions of the Court (considered in Chapter IX), one in 1962 and the other in 1963, have made it increasingly difficult for the public schools to deal with religion in conventional ways. The 1962 decision, generally known as the Regents' Prayer Case, concerned a state-sponsored optional prayer for use in the public schools of New York state. The prayer, arrived at after months of discussion by representatives of many religious groups, was simple:

> Almighty God, we acknowledge our dependence upon Thee, and we beg Thy blessings upon us, our parents, our teachers and our country.

[3] From *God in Education: A New Opportunity for American Schools,* by Niels C. Nielsen, Jr. (New York: Sheed and Ward, 1966), pp. 26-27.
[4] This and information following summarized from *The Bible, Religion, and the Public Schools,* by Donald E. Boles (Ames, Iowa: Iowa State University Press, 1963).

Soon after the prayer began to be used in the New Hyde Park School District, action was initiated to prevent its use, the case eventually reaching the United States Supreme Court. That court ruled, six to one, that the use of the prayer was unconstitutional.

The 1963 case pertains to Bible reading and the recitation of the Lord's Prayer in Abington Township, Pennsylvania, according to a Pennsylvania requirement that ten verses from the Bible be read each day. Such reading having been held unconstitutional by a federal district court in 1960, the case eventually reached the United States Supreme Court, which agreed with the lower court. Basing his opinion especially on the "Establishment Clause" of the Constitution, Mr. Justice Clark also argued that such an official religious exercise might be interpreted as interfering with the "free exercise of religion."

We noted in Chapter IX, however, that Mr. Justice Clark in the 1963 decision made explicit not only the *possibility* but also the *desirability* of the schools' including a study of religions in their curriculum. (A part of his opinion is quoted in Chapter IX.) It should be pointed out, also, that the decisions of the Court have been especially directed against any hint of the schools *establishing* religion or religious practices. This prohibition exists in relation both to existing religions (Christianity, for example, or any of its forms) or to a "school religion" (such as the New York prayer has been accused of being).

There has been considerable criticism of the decisions, especially of the New York prayer case. The chief argument for the decision is that the prayer prescribed by the Board of Regents very nearly established a religion, even though such establishment was contained only in a simple prayer. The chief argument against this decision and many of the others is that all of them tend to set up secularism as the religion of public schools. That is, if those who oppose any expression of religion in the schools prevail, the schools either by implication (or even explicitly) tend to encourage a nontheistic interpretation of life and history.

Indeed the issue is really not whether prayer is offered in

167

the schools—this is actually a minor matter. The crucial issue is the orientation of the curriculum. If it is secularistic in its approach to life—that is, concerned only with immediate ends and values—then the tendency is for the curriculum to encourage secularism. If this be so, the process of secularization has progressed to the point where secularism is a rival religion to the historic ones. This statement assumes that when the process of *secularization* (to use the distinction made by Winter, Cox, and others and noted in Chapter V) has reached the stage of *secularism*, it may be identified as a kind of religion.

Regardless of what one may think of the decisions, however, they are not likely to be reversed soon. The immediate response of the churches, working with the schools as well as independently, is, therefore, to seek ways (1) of encouraging the schools to do what they can more legitimately and effectively do—teach *about* religions—and (2) of supplementing what the schools are able to do. Since our concern in this book is not just with historical understanding as an end in itself but also with the study and the teaching of history, we must consider how history can be dealt with so as to fulfill the two conditions just stated.

## RELIGION AND PUBLIC EDUCATION: SOME PROPOSALS

As background to a consideration of how the churches can deal with history in relation to public education, we must first look at some of the options that have been either tried or projected with regard to religion and public education. Although not all of these plans are of direct interest to us, some of the leading proposals are listed in order that matters of specific interest may be seen in perspective. The first two are means by which religious groups participate directly in general education; the next three are means by which the public schools may participate in the religious culture; the final three are ways in which religious groups are able to supplement what the public schools do.

1. *The Christian day school,* or the parochial school, as it is

known in Roman Catholicism, is a live and, in some groups, a growing option. It was the original aim of Roman Catholicism to provide education for all its children and youth in church-controlled schools. The Missouri Synod Lutherans and Seventh-Day Adventists also have for some years sought to develop church-oriented day schools for their constituencies. The Protestant Episcopal Church has been less ambitious but nevertheless active in the establishment of such schools, which are usually largely nonsectarian. Within recent years, church day schools, usually supported by the more conservative churches, have mushroomed. Although some of these schools avowedly have been begun to circumvent desegregation and others have been started partly for this reason, the result has been a great increase in Protestant school enrollment.[5]

Roman Catholicism is facing its parochial school system with less enthusiasm than it once did. Father Neil G. McCluskey noted in *Commonweal* as long ago as 1964 that two general conclusions were finding wide acceptance: Catholics are coming to see that the ideal of "every Catholic child in a Catholic school" is an impossible utopia; while non-Catholics are accepting the fact that parochial schools are a significant part of American education, whether desirable or not.[6]

The acceptance by mainline Protestantism of church-related schools as the most desirable possibility is unlikely. Although such schools may freely include religion in their total curricular and extracurricular life, they face many problems of financing, staffing, finding adequate textbooks, maintaining high academic standards. Such problems as these not only have made many Roman Catholics rethink their system; they make most Protestants hesitant about beginning such a system.

2. *Dual enrollment* is the term adopted by the National Council of Churches as a more appropriate designation for a plan for some years called "shared time." Whereas the old

[5] See "Will Protestant Church Schools Become a Third Force," by Henry A. Buchanan and Bob W. Brown, *Christianity Today*, May 12, 1967, pp. 787-89.

[6] See "A Changing Pattern," by Neil G. McCluskey, *Commonweal*, March, 1964, p. 507.

term, *shared time,* implied that the child's school day belonged to the public schools and might be shared with the churches for Christian education, *dual enrollment* views the time as the child's and his parents'. Thus he may legitimately be enrolled part time in both a public school and in a church day school.

Dual enrollment may be seen from two points of view. From the perspective of the already existing church day school, the student takes some of his courses (for example, science, mathematics, shop, home economics, and the like) in the public school while he remains enrolled also in the church school. From the perspective of the public school, the student takes some courses (for example, religion, literature, history, and the like) in the church day school. Because the student, however, is enrolled in both schools, the plan is different from released time, which will be discussed later. Supporters of dual enrollment vary in their expectation of what courses should be offered by the church school; they range from only courses in religion as a separate subject to a variety of courses especially related to religious thought.

Although the reaction to dual enrollment, or shared time, has been mixed, there has been a great deal of interest in the plan. Roman Catholics and those Protestant groups that have day schools have more to gain immediately, since the plan would relieve the financial pressure under which such schools usually operate. Not all Roman Catholics are in favor, however; nor is there a common mind among Protestants. Many fear that such a plan would be divisive, since they feel that any attempt at education by the church will be sectarian.

3. *Teaching about religion* is the alternative proposed by Mr. Justice Clark in his majority opinion in the Abington Case in 1963, as we have already seen. Previously a number of groups and individuals had discussed the possibility of what was often called the "objective teaching of religion." [7] This

[7] See, for example, two volumes from the American Council on Education: *The Relation of Religion to Public Education: The Basic Principles* (Washington, 1947) and *The Function of the Public Schools in Dealing with Religion* (Washington, 1953); also a volume of the Educational Policies Commission of the National Education Association and the American Association of School Administrators, *Moral and Spiritual Values in the Public Schools.* (Washington: National Education Associa-

phrase has proved an unfortunate one, since it is highly improbable, as we have seen, that teaching can be objective. To be preferred is the one that is now most often used, "teaching about religion."

That it is possible to deal with organized religion as a part of the subject matter of the public schools is obvious, since such teaching does happen. Instances were pointed out in some of the textbooks analyzed in Chapter IX. The material devoted to religion is not extensive, is often one sided, and may not be interestingly presented. It appears in many texts, however, at least to a limited extent.

We may not have applied to the subject matter of religion the same care we have given to political matters, themselves controversial in many instances. Future historians, for example, should have no more difficulty in dealing with the religious life of the twentieth century than with the Arab-Israeli situation. Responsible teaching requires that all controversial matters be included in the teaching of history.

We may not be willing, however, to allow maximum free inquiry in the public schools. If not, then the institutions of a free society may be in jeopardy, and the quality of education must be seriously questioned. If the schools cannot be free to deal responsibly with religion as a part of the cultural heritage of the past and of life in the present, serious questions must be raised with respect to both the comprehensive nature and the quality of such education.

4. We have moved to a fourth approach to our problem, which is not a solution but a way of arriving at one. Robert Lynn, of Union Theological Seminary in New York City, fears the blandness of much public education. The chief contribution of the churches to public education, he says, may be their efforts *to encourage the public schools to deal with all kinds of controversial issues, including religion.* He writes:

> The study of religion in the public schools will become competent only when the educator is free and

tion, 1951) ; also *Religion in the Public Schools*, a report of the American Association of School Administrators (New York: Harper Chapel Books, 1964) .

willing to exercise his rightful independence from community pressure. Our first intent, therefore, is to help the school be a school and not the frightened shadow of American society. And our first need, therefore, is for informed critics who can demonstrate the intricate relationships between academic freedom, the development of a true profession among public school educators, and the ability to handle explosive issues in the classroom.[8]

We are not likely in the near future to reach the degree of freedom Lynn desires, though improvement should be possible if means can be found for helping teachers know how to deal freely and responsibly with controversial subjects.

5. A fifth position, difficult to designate, is held by Philip H. Phenix, professor of the philosophy of education at Teachers College, Columbia University. It is closely related to the larger effort described in Chapter V—that is, to discern the presence of God in the whole of life. Phenix, who is trained both as educator and as theologian, suggests the possibility of dealing with religion in the public schools from the perspective of three purposes: (1) "to understand better what is believed and practiced in traditional religion"; (2) "to reflect constructively and critically about these traditions"; and (3) "to see the relevance of various religious ideas to the understanding of 'secular' concerns comprehensively and in depth." [9]

We have just dealt with the substance of Phenix's first and second purposes. The third relates to the finding of "religious" meaning in the "secular." Later we shall look at how history can be understood in this manner; for the moment, let us try to understand in general what he means.

It is clear that Phenix's thought is closely related to that of the secular theologians of our time, that is, those who em-

---

[8] From *Protestant Strategies in Education,* by Robert W. Lynn (New York: Association Press, 1964), p. 80.

[9] From *Education and the Worship of God,* by Philip H. Phenix (Philadelphia: The Westminster Press, 1966), p. 30. A more extensive presentation of Phenix's point of view is found in his *Realms of Meaning: A Philosophy of the Curriculum for General Education* (New York: McGraw-Hill Book Company, 1964).

phasize the importance of responding to the reality of God in all of man's existence, not just in those realms normally thought of as "religious." This means, Phenix says, a rejection of nature and supernature as two separate realms of reality. When the two are separated, we imply that God is in those matters we cannot explain but is not present in what we understand. On the contrary, says Phenix, every natural object "is a potential source of limitless riches of meaning, and every ordinary temporal event may be regarded from the perspective of eternity." (Page 31, *Education and the Worship of God*.)

Many Christians find it hard to understand this perspective, for we have not taken our heritage seriously at this point. Hebrew thought knows no separation of sacred and secular, and the categories of nature and supernature have been imposed on biblical thought from a postscientific perspective. Perhaps the most understandable way of putting what Phenix means is to talk about seeing God in the natural world. In a previous era, that of liberal theology, much was said about finding God in nature. In a postliberal period, this approach was largely overshadowed in the church by the emphasis (presented in Chapter IV) on the uniqueness of holy history. In today's so-called secular theology, an attempt is being made to recover the insight of liberal theology, though hopefully within the context, or from the perspective, of the revelation of God in Jesus Christ.

What Phenix proposes, then, is that students be helped to find meaning in areas of the curriculum we normally think of as secular. In his extensive discussion of the curriculum for public education, *Realms of Meaning*, he proposes that the organizing principle for the curriculum be *meaning*, that education be grounded in the search for meaning, and that its aim be thought of as "to promote the growth of meaning." [10] Insofar as education contributes to the growth of meaning, it is religious. Whether such meaning is labeled with traditional Christian terminology is not the crucial issue for Phenix, as

[10] From *Realms of Meaning: A Philosophy of the Curriculum for General Education*, p. 25. See also pp. 5-49.

it is not for the secular theologians. Rather, the experience of the meaning itself—through literature or history, for example —is the important thing.

Let us look again at the example of repentance and new life found in Arthur Miller's play *Death of a Salesman*. The question—which I believe Phenix would answer negatively— is: Is Biff's experience of self-recognition and new life any less genuine because he did not identify it in traditional Christian terms?

For the moment, we shall leave Phenix's proposal; but we shall return to it later to examine it for its possibility of interpreting history in the public schools.

6. Thus far our proposals have involved either the church's organizing its own school system totally or in part, or the school's assuming responsibility for dealing with religion within the bounds of constitutional provisions. We turn now to three means whereby the church can *supplement* the teaching of the public schools. The examples under the general classifications are illustrative, not definitive.

The most common, though not necessarily the most effective, is the *Sunday church school*. Its advantages include the large number of children and youth already attending its sessions—more than attend any other organized teaching activity of the church. The Sunday school is well established in most congregations, and most of the major communions have recently spent millions of dollars to provide upgraded materials for their church schools.

Whether, as one commentator a few years ago stated in *Life,* the Sunday school is the most wasted hour of the week is a matter of debate. That it represents a "marginal enterprise," as Robert Lynn, in his *Protestant Strategies in Education,* has called Protestant religious education, seems clear. It usually allows at most for one hour of teaching; many of its teachers are relatively untrained; and attendance is at best irregular. Although some communions are now seeking to increase the time for study to two hours per week, to do so will usually require scheduling church school sessions at some time other than the conventional Sunday school hour.

With all of its built-in problems, however, the Sunday

church school provides at least a minimum opportunity for Christian education. Its work might be more effective if a serious effort were made to relate its curriculum to that of the public schools. Doing so would require more initiative than most congregations now assume; for, as we saw regarding social studies curricula, the curriculum offerings across the nation are anything but uniform.

7. The problems associated with Sunday morning for Christian teaching suggest the necessity of looking to the weekday or weekend for other possible times; our next church-oriented proposal, therefore, is *weekday Christian education.*

The most common church weekday enterprise is the vacation church school, in existence since the early 1900's. Also common have been various kinds of summer institutes, assemblies, and camps for youth. More recently, camping for older children has been instituted, as has family camping. The weekend occasion for young people in the church has increasingly come to the fore. Some people feel that some such setting for Christian education may become the most profitable one for the teaching of young people.

After-school classes for children are carried out in some localities, and churches attempting such education have sometimes been surprised at parents' willingness to cooperate. This has been especially the case with confirmation classes. Churches might well consider extending the programs of after-school classes. The Through-the-Week Christian Education Curriculum of the National Council of Churches, for which this book provides background, is an effort to provide a curriculum for week-day classes.

Very little has been done, however, to correlate such teaching with that of the public schools. By and large, the curriculum for such occasions has been so completely church oriented that such correlation would be nearly impossible. Is it not possible, however, that with children and youth so fully oriented to the public schools, more valuable church school learning might occur if a direct relationship could be made with what they are learning in public school? Would it be possible to go even a step further to use the same materials that are being used in the public schools in certain courses, viewing them from the additional perspective of the church? We shall have more to say of this proposal in our discussion of the teaching of history.

8. A final possibility is *released time*. We have already noted that religious instruction held during school hours in the school building was ruled unconstitutional in 1948 but was allowed by a subsequent decision, in 1952, off the school premises. In some states, enabling legislation makes released-time classes a live option.

This setting has disadvantages, also. When the released-time period is at the end of the school day, boys and girls are more likely to create discipline problems unless the teacher is an unusually good one. The subject matter in released-time classes is usually unrelated to what has gone on during the remainder of the day, requiring the children to shift gears completely in their orientation. Too often, also, fully qualified and skilled teachers are not available. Nevertheless, released time offers one more opportunity, where such classes are possible, for Christian teaching.

## THE TEACHING OF HISTORY

Thus far we have looked at some of the proposals for relating religion to public education without specific reference to the subject with which we are concerned—namely, history. We shall now look specifically at what is involved in the teaching of history in the settings that have been described. The numbers below refer to the settings so numbered in the preceding discussion.

*1 and 2.* Since the teaching of history would be the same were it occurring in a Christian day school or in the church portion of a dual-enrollment plan, these two settings will be considered together. Although they are not viable possibilities for most of us now, they are related to the larger subject of this book and hence will be discussed briefly. What is involved in the teaching of history in a church day school?

It should be obvious that the teacher in such a setting is first of all obligated to be fair in his presentation of history. We have noted earlier the extent to which perspective colors interpretation and that all reporting involves interpretation. The church-oriented historian ought to be especially careful to be fair to differing points of view, to different reports of the same incident—in other words, to be as truthful as possible about the past.

The teaching of history will, of course, include facts about the history of organized religion and the way in which it is related to general history. One may be tempted to stop at this point, thinking that he has thus fulfilled his obligation. As we have seen, the public schools can do this kind of teaching; and doubtless they would do more of it were they encouraged to do so. In the church-oriented school, of course, a particular religious group can present its own history in a detailed way, as the public school cannot. Even so, however, this approach to teaching history is incomplete from the Christian perspective.

Still another aspect of the church's teaching of history has to do with perspective. Such teaching should make clear the basically Christian understanding of history. These assumptions (considered in earlier chapters) should be made explicit. Comparison with other perspectives helps to illuminate the one being presented.

Beyond this general kind of teaching, a serious attempt can be made to look at all of history as the arena of God's activity and self-revelation. To put it in Phenix's terms, the study of history may become the occasion for the worship of God. Indeed, such serious study is "fundamentally religious not only because of its disclosure of the full significance of time and creation but further because of its relation to the search for meaning." [11] Whether or not this type of study is a possibility for the public schools is debatable; that it ought to be a part of the teaching done in the church-oriented school seems clear.

Such teaching requires textbooks that interpret the God-dimension of all existence. It also presupposes teachers who understand history from the perspective of God's concern for an involvement in all of life. Although I would be unrealistic

[11] From *Education and the Worship of God*, by Philip H. Phenix, p. 147.

in suggesting that this kind of teaching can be done easily, I do not feel that it is impossible, provided the education of history teachers includes basic theological understanding.

*3 and 4.* We have said enough about the inclusion of material about religious groups in the teaching of history to indicate that this way of treating religion in the public schools is possible, even though the problems concerning such teaching continue. Those problems involve, for example, the lack of understanding of religion on the part of many history teachers and the difficulty of dealing with a controversial subject such as religion.

It seems clear, then, that study and experimentation in regard to teaching about religion in the public schools should continue and be expanded. Two issues require special attention if the situation is to improve. First, teacher education must include instruction in the meaning and history of religion. With an increasing number of state universities establishing departments of religion, this kind of education now becomes possible. In a survey made of 376 four-year colleges in 1956-58, 33 per cent of the total offered such courses; but only 12 per cent of the teachers' colleges did so.[12] Much, therefore, needs to be done in regard to the teaching of religion on the college level. Part of teacher education ought also to include help in dealing with controversial subjects openly, fairly, and without arousing undue hostility.

The second issue has to do with textbooks. So influential are textbooks on the content of courses that, unless they deal adequately with issues of organized religion, the work of the class is considerably handicapped. It may be necessary in preparing texts on history to enlist the help of scholars representing several points of view about religion; perhaps to quote them instead of summarizing; and otherwise to provide a maximum amount of material which interprets in some depth basic ideas of various religious groups.

Robert Lynn's proposal that the schools be freed to deal with controversial issues needs to be noted only briefly. In

[12] See *The Education of Historians in the United States,* by Dexter Perkins, John L. Snell, *et al.* (New York: McGraw-Hill Book Company, 1962) , p. 77.

fewer areas is such freedom more badly needed than in history and social studies. History could be made both more exciting and more meaningful if teachers of the subject were freed to deal with all kinds of controversial questions, including religion. As we have suggested, freedom to do so would require training of teachers to handle such content responsibly. Until Lynn's proposal is taken more seriously, the public school teaching of history will remain too much a shadow of the fears, divisions, and pressures that constitute a large part of contemporary life.

5. We turn now to Phenix's proposal that history should be taught in depth, and therefore in its religious dimension, in the public schools. I am not optimistic that this proposal can be completely and immediately implemented. Sufficient value inheres in it, however, both for the church and for the future of public education, that it deserves more careful analysis than we have thus far given it.

Phenix sees history as a disclosure of the Way of God. Language is interpreted as the Word of God, science as the Wisdom of God, and ethics as the Will of God. In the study of history, as in all study, it is not the particular subject matter involved that makes such study religious. What makes the study of history an experience of worship "is that it be performed with such joyful seriousness and devotion that inner depths of meaning are opened up, manifesting the presence and power of the creative source of being." [13]

The primary religious reality of history is found in response to the wonder of time. Since the context in which all the events of history occur is time, what matters religiously "is the response the student makes to the deep mysteries of time" (page 145). "History is the story of creation," Phenix writes. "It is the recital of what human beings have done to originate casual sequences." He goes on to say:

> On this account, history is also a disclosure of man's spiritual nature whereby he participates in the divine creative action. If God is the ground of all being, and if

[13] From *Education and the Worship of God*, p. 139. The next several page references in the text are to this book.

179

from the activity of free human agents new being is generated, it follows that persons in their exercise of freedom share in the divine creative life. This is the principal reason for asserting that the study of history by one who takes the reality of time, freedom, and creation seriously constitutes an occasion for the worship of God (page 146).

History is not only the story of creation, Phenix goes on to say; it is also the story of re-creation. This historian re-enacts in imagination the events of the past, thus bringing them into meaningful relation with the present. As this process takes place, persons in the present become involved in decisions of the past. The teacher of history, if he performs his task with dedication and insight, thus helps the student participate in the creativity that was present in the original acts.

Historical inquiry also raises questions of meaning. More than any other subject, history requires the pursuit of meaning ("that which makes sense out of life"). Although there are various ways of interpreting the meaning of history, Phenix feels that most important is dealing with "the significance of unique events, caused by the creative action of free human agents" (page 151). The purpose in studying history is to become identified with events in such a way that they are re-created in the present. As this re-creation occurs, man begins to view life from something of the perspective from which God views human existence (page 152).

The chief sin of man, Phenix says, is "his self-concern and his preoccupation with his own security and satisfaction." As a person becomes involved in history, he is released from this "self-regarding condition and given the opportunity to enter freely and disinterestedly into the lives of others, who, because they are not contemporary, cannot figure as factors in the calculation of his present advantage" (page 153). As one becomes concerned with understanding those about whom he reads in history, he shares in the love of God for his creatures (page 153).

In other words, a study of history can release a person from his own self-concern, broaden his understanding of life, and enlarge his perspective so that he shares in God's concern for all of creation, past and present. The wonder and mystery of man and his actions are illuminated by a serious study of history. The depths of man's being—his capacity for both good and evil—are revealed through a study of the past. John Smith, of Main Street, USA, can participate in the totality of man's existence if only he can be shaken out of the particularity of his own existence and made to share in the universality of human existence.

Perhaps a personal illustration will be helpful. One of the most illuminating studies of history in which I have engaged is participation in the "sound and light" technique developed in the Loire Valley in France in the 1950's. This technique combines light and sound to enliven some period of history. As some part of the physical remainder of history is illuminated—a chateau or the pyramids, for example—a recorded voice recounts significant events associated with that object. As I listened to the history of ancient Egypt while I sat in the desert before the lighted face of the Sphinx, that history became real and personal. The history of the Parthenon in Athens and of the Forum in Rome became almost as personal as my own family history. Thus as history came alive, I was released to some extent from my own petty perspective and became a participant in the past. At the same time, the sweep of the past made me a participant in God's time rather than in just my own.

There is nothing religious in the conventional sense about these experiences, but their effect on me was religious. This must be something of what Phenix has in mind when he says history studied in depth has religious implications.

The position Phenix supports has been presented in some detail for two reasons: first, it appears to be consistent with the general perspective I have maintained in previous chapters; and second, it is a serious attempt to show how the perspective of previous chapters can be implemented in the study and teaching of history. Although Phenix has not worked out all the implications of his theory, his approach serves as the basis for continuing inquiry concerning the religious possibilities of public education.

## THE NEED FOR CORRELATION

*6, 7, and 8.* The last three settings to be considered are similar in that all of them involve church-centered teaching and thus are under the control of the churches. Each has its own disadvantages, some of which were considered in the section prior to this one. All of them now include some study of church history in all communions. In some instances, the biblical understanding of history is presented, and the larger understanding of God's relationship to all of life has found its way into curriculum materials.

By and large, however, there has been little attempt to relate church teaching to public school curricula. Nor is there agreement concerning how much of such correlation is either desirable or possible. In view of the problems connected with relating religion directly to public education, it would appear high time for Christian educators to give more attention to the possibility of such correlation.

One of the problems in attempting to relate church school teaching to public school learnings, as we saw in Chapter IX, is the lack of uniformity in course offerings. Where the elective system is allowed (as it is in many schools), the grades at which students may take particular subjects may vary within a given school. Textbooks in the same subject do not follow the same or even similar outlines. This diversity is not to be regretted but, rather, is to be welcomed; for there is too much uniformity of thought in the public schools. Indeed, if programs of study were made to fit the needs of particular students (as in some of the better systems), there would be even less similarity of course content than there now is.

In view of such differences, no one set of curriculum materials will be appropriate for all situations. Where a set curriculum is used, therefore, it must be adapted for the particular public school pattern or patterns followed by the students in the congregation. If public school materials are to be considered in the church's teaching, the teacher or some supervisory person must secure the materials used by the schools and adapt church materials for maximum correlation. This may make possible only an occasional correlation of church and public school curricula, fairly common correlation, or, in rare instances, rather complete melding of the two.

A more radical but, I believe, a sounder proposal involves the use in church education of the materials used in public education. For example, world history is a common subject in either the ninth or the tenth grade. Under a skilled teacher, it would be possible for ninth- or tenth-grade students to use their textbook in world history in a church class but to use it with a different emphasis. For example, supplementary material would be needed about the various religions of the world. Hebrew history would be incorporated into the study of the civilizations of the eastern Mediterranean. Early Christian history would be considered in more detail in relation to Roman history, as would the Reformation in relation to the histories of the several European nations in which the Reformation flowered.

Above and beyond factual material, an attempt would be made to interpret history from a Christian perspective. There is danger of artificiality at this point, to be sure. This kind of teaching requires considerable knowledge and skill, and it is probable that we do not at the present have teachers adequately prepared for it. If we are to do a more responsible job in the future, however, we must not allow the difficulties of implementing a plan to discourage us from giving it a serious try.

Perhaps in the future, curriculum building on a church-wide or interchurch basis will emphasize resources for curriculum-making by a congregation or other church groups, rather than student books and teaching plans for sessions. This approach requires a greater degree of sophistication and willingness to be creative on the part of congregations than now exists in most places. For the time being, a less ambitious means of correlation will be followed by most congregations.

## CHURCH AND PUBLIC SCHOOL TEACHING

Regardless of the particular materials used in church classes, however, three kinds of supplementary resources are needed in relating the church curriculum to that of the public school.

First, there is that which is factual and interpretative. This includes data on the events of church history and of religions other than Christianity. It includes an interpretation of history from the biblical perspective and a consideration of the impingement of history on organized religion.

Second, a Christian perspective on all of history can be provided. Something of the approach defined in earlier chapters is what I have in mind: history is not self-contained; it has meaning, which comes ultimately from God; it moves toward something—that is, it is eschatological, or it awaits its fulfillment under God. Problems such as those considered in Chapters VI, VII, and VIII of the present work may also be included. As a part of such a consideration, the biblical perspective on life and history will, of course, occupy a significant place.

Third, the interpretation of all of history from a Christian perspective should make clear that God is related to all of life and history, not just to holy history or the areas of life generally thought of as religious. This is the perspective included in Chapter V. It is the point of view put forward by Philip Phenix regarding the religious dimension of public education. It does not mean so much that history will be viewed as a "grand plan" of which God is sovereign, since it is not at all clear to most human beings precisely what this plan is. Rather, it consists of helping persons become aware of God as the source of all life and being and of the fact that men may respond to God, either consciously or unconsciously, without necessarily using traditional Christian terminology.

If life is not to continue to be divided into the sacred and the secular, it is absolutely necessary that what the student learns in the bulk of his educational experience not be isolated from his learning in the realm of the religious. So long as sacred history is completely separated from the secular in the education of children and youth, a special effort is required to help them see the connection between the two. If it is not possible—as I suspect it is not at the present—to introduce Phenix's proposal into public education, then the live alternative is for the church to do supplementary work. The most

184

crucial aspect of this task is to help the student perceive the reality of God in all of life and history.

It should be made clear, however, that this proposal does not call for a strained interpretation which sees a burning bush in every happening. Nor is it suggested that events be interpreted falsely, allowing the interpreter to find in them what he wishes. Indeed, one of the ways in which history becomes a religious undertaking is for the historian to be rigorously honest. Such honesty does not allow the historian to attribute categorically to God's intervention events that may be simply a matter of chance. He may make clear, however, that a person or a group of people did see in a historical event the hand of God, as the Hebrews did in the deliverance from Egypt, and that their understanding colored the rest of their history.

There is just as much reason, however, for seeing God's activity in an event which is not so interpreted by the participant. For example, the valedictorian of the 1967 Harvard Law School graduating class was Joe Sorrentino. Here was a young man, then thirty years old, who had flunked out of high school four times, been a street fighter in Brooklyn and a veteran of more than 100 rumbles, failed at various jobs, and was, at the end of his first enlistment in the Marines, discharged with a general rather than an honorable discharge. Then Joe Sorrentino began his comeback, including another enlistment in the Marines with an honorable discharge and highest honors in graduation from high school and college. Finally he achieved the highest average in his class at Harvard Law School.

Many people might wish that Joe Sorrentino had made some kind of traditional religious interpretation of the radical change in his life, but he did not. In his valedictory address, he concluded, instead, with these words: " 'Do not look for love, tragedy or trauma to explain this change. It was simply resolution from within'—and, he added, proof that 'in America such things are possible.' " [14]

Is it possible to give a religious interpretation in the sense

[14] From "The Dropout Who Made Good," *Time*, June 30, 1967, p. 59.

that the secular theologians and Phenix view life? I think so, for, in spite of what might be interpreted as a kind of brashness in Sorrentino's statement, it is also possible to interpret his achievement as an example of the amazing creativity of man. And if one really believes that man is God's creature, endowed with a derived creativity, one can then see in this event a striking example of the reality and creativity of the divine.

There are, of course, problems connected with the interpretation, for the event must be seen in relationship to the whole problem of evil. Why Joe Sorrentino escaped from his past and why many people do not must also be taken into account. There is mystery here not only in terms of the inner motivation of Joe Sorrentino but also in the lack of such motivation in the lives of countless others. There are no simple explanations in life, as our previous chapters have shown us. The important matter, however, is for us to be able to discern the reality of God with or without complete explanations.

The discussion of this third type of material needed to supplement the public school teaching of history has grown too long. The importance of helping children and youth see the divine dimension in all of life justifies our repeated consideration of this matter, however. It is, I believe, the chief antidote to the secularism threatening to become a substitute for Christian faith in our time. So long as we separate religious teaching from teaching about the whole of life, we are in danger of failing to help students see that all of life, not just some particular aspects of it, is God's.

All that which works for the good of man can and must be interpreted as the working of the hidden Christ. Where there is concern for and acceptance of persons; where there is an affirmation of life; where there is truth and integrity—there and in countless other similar places, we can in faith discern the action of God. The purpose of this third aspect of the teaching of history is to help persons discern the hidden Christ (or the reality of God) present in all creation and all human existence. The Christian affirms that without this hidden reality of God there would be no creation and no human history.

## CONCLUSION

The person who views history from the Christian perspective does not come to historic events with a blank mind; the Christian comes to history, we hope, with an open mind, open to the depths of meaning in all events—those that have traditionally been considered secular as well as those that have been called sacred.

The Christian comes to these events believing that they are meaningful, but the events are not self-interpreting. He sees those events in terms of the background of his Hebrew forebears, whose self-identity was forged out of the ordeal of centuries of travail through an increasing awareness of God. The Christian brings to history, as to life, the self-awareness that comes from God's self-revelation in Jesus Christ. He understands history from the perspective of the original events of that revelation and the centuries of reflection on it, and he reacts to continuing revelation in relation to those events.

The Christian recognizes that the problems of life and history are not easy to solve, that they are, in fact, not easily explained. But he finds a clue to their meaning in Jesus Christ; and he participates in, and, in the light of this basic faith, reflects upon, events he only dimly understands.

The Christian's perception of the reality of God is not confined to his own personal history, however, for he recognizes that God is also the God of all creation. Christ is not always known by name, but the hidden Christ is present in all of life and history. It is the responsibility of the Christian to heighten his perception of the reality of God to include all of life, and he will rejoice in the fact that men of various faiths or of no religion at all are instruments of the living God.

If such a person happens to be a teacher of history, he will recognize his responsibility for communicating this perspective to his students. The teaching of factual material alone is not the teaching of history but is instruction in a chronicle that may or may not be accurate. As the teacher of history takes his vocation seriously and as he looks with concern and insight into the past, he will be taking the first step toward teaching *history*. As he is able to do so, his interpretation should

187

broaden to include not only events and causes, but also the meaning of history itself.

The study of history is an academic pursuit calling for skills, knowledge of the past, and the ability to pursue research in a competent manner. The historian's first responsibility is to be a good historian, that is, to use the tools of his craft in the pursuit of knowledge. To make of history nothing more than an academic pursuit, however, is to miss both the excitement and the deeper values of historical study. To know history is to know human existence, and to know human existence is to begin to know the meaning of life. The purpose of history is partly to illumine life's meaning, to give it broader perspective, and to deepen perception of the present.

As we study the past, we shall, on the one hand, be led to see the pettiness of our own exaggerated self-concern. On the other hand, if we are sensitive to the interrelatedness of persons, events, and the continuity of life, we shall recognize that, though we are only one person, we *are one*.

We shall need the perspective of the One whom we name "the hinge of history," however, lest we fall into despair concerning the insignificance of our own small life. Each person means something to God. From the long view of history, faith and faith alone makes such a statement possible.

Man individually and men together count: this is the enduring message of the gospel. It is the perspective from which the gospel views both history and the individual life. In more conventional terms, the gospel proclaims God's love for man. It asks for man's faithful, loving service to God and neighbor.

Three conclusions concerning history overarch its unanswered questions. The first is from Longfellow's translation of the seventeenth-century German poet, Friedrich von Logau; the second is from William Cowper's hymn-poem of the eighteenth century; and the third is from Luke 12:48a.

"Though the mills of God grind slowly, yet they
    grind exceeding small."

"God moves in a mysterious way His wonders to perform."

"Every one to whom much is given, of him much will
    be required."

# SELECTED READINGS

Allport, Gordon. *Becoming: Basic Considerations for a Psychology of Personality*. New Haven: Yale University Press, 1955.

Allport, Gordon. *Personality: A Psychological Interpretation*. New York: Henry Holt & Co., 1937.

Allport, Gordon. *The Nature of Predudice*. Boston: Addison-Wesley; paper abridged ed., Doubleday, 1954.

American Association of School Administrators. *Religion in the Public Schools*. New York: Harper Chapel Books, 1964, 1965.

Baillie, John. *The Idea of Revelation in Recent Thought*. New York: Columbia University Press, 1956.

Beggs, David W., and R. Bruce McQuigg. *America's Schools and Churches: Partners in Conflict*. Bloomington: Indiana University Press, 1965.

Bell, Daniel, Ed. *The Radical Right*. Garden City: Doubleday (Anchor Books), 1963, 1964.

Bennett, John C. *Christianity and Communism Today*. New York: Association Press (Reflection Book Giant), 1962.

Berlin, Isaiah. *Historical Inevitability*. London: Oxford University Press, 1954.

Blau, Joseph L., ed. *Cornerstones of Religious Freedom in America*. New York: Peter Smith, Publisher. Rev. ed., 1964.

Boles, Donald E. *The Bible, Religion, and the Public Schools*. Ames, Iowa: Iowa State University Press, 1961, 1963. 3rd ed., 1965.

Bonhoeffer, Dietrich. *Letters and Papers from Prison*. (Published originally in America as *Prisoner for God*.) New York: The Macmillan Company. Cloth, 1967; paper, 1962.

Boulding, Kenneth E. *Conflict and Defense: A General Theory*. New York: Harper Torchbooks, 1962, 1963.

Braaten, Carl E. *New Directions in Theology Today*: Vol. II, *History and Hermeneutics*. Philadelphia: The Westminster Press, 1966.

Brown, Samuel Windsor. *The Secularization of American Education* (Teachers College, Columbia University Contributions to Education, No. 49). New York: Teachers College, Columbia University, 1912.

Bugental, James F. T., ed. *Challenges of Humanistic Psychology*. New York: McGraw-Hill Book Company, 1967.

Butterfield, Herbert. *Christianity and History*. New York: Charles Scribner's Sons, 1949, 1950, 1960.

Carr. E. H. *What Is History?* London: Macmillan and Company, 1961.

Carr. Edwin R. *The Social Studies*. New York: The Center for Applied Research in Education, Inc., 1965.

Cartwright, William H., and Richard L. Watson, Jr., eds. *Interpreting and Teaching American History*. Thirty-First Yearbook of the National Council for the Social Studies, National Education Association, 1201 Sixteenth Street, N.W., Washington, D.C. 20036, 1961.

Casserley, J. V. Langmead. *Toward a Theology of History*. New York: Holt, Rinehart and Winston, 1965.

Collingswood, R. G. *The Idea of History*. New York: Oxford University Press (Galaxy Book), 1946, 1956. Ed. by T. M. Knox.

Cox, Harvey. *The Secular City*. New York: The Macmillan Company, 1966.

Dray, William H. *Philosophy of History*. Englewood Cliffs, N.J.: Prentice-Hall. Cloth, 1964; paper, 1967.

Dunn, William Kailer. *What Happened to Religious Education?* Baltimore: The Johns Hopkins Press, 1958.

*Encyclopedia Americana*. New York: Grolier Educational Corp., 1966.

Engle, Shirley H., ed. *New Perspectives in World History*. Thirty-Fourth Yearbook of the National Council for the Social Studies, National Education Association, 1201 Sixteenth Street, N.W., Washington, D.C. 20036, 1964.

Fennell, William O. "The Theology of True Secularity," in *New Theology No. 2*, Martin E. Marty and Dean G. Peerman, eds. New York: The Macmillan Company, 1965.

Friedlander, Anna Fay. *The Shared Time Strategy*. St. Louis: Concordia Publishing House, 1966.

Fromm, Erich. *Escape from Freedom*. New York: Holt, Rinehart, and Winston, 1941.

Fromm, Erich. *The Heart of Man*. New York: Harper & Row, 1964.

Harrington, Michael. *The Other America: Poverty in the United States.* New York: The Macmillan Company, 1962.

Harris, Judah J. *The Treatment of Religion in Elementary School Social Studies Textbooks.* New York: Anti-Defamation League of B'nai B'rith, 1963.

Harvey, Van A. *A Handbook of Theological Terms.* New York: The Macmillan Company, 1966.

Harvey, Van A. *The Historian and the Believer.* New York: The Macmillan Company, 1966.

Haselden, Kyle. *The Racial Problem in Christian Perspective.* New York: Harper & Brothers, 1959.

*Homefront.* Monthly paper published by the Institute for American Democracy, 1330 Massachusetts Avenue, N.W., Washington, D.C. 20005.

Hook, Sidney, ed. *Determinism and Freedom in the Age of Modern Science.* New York: New York University Press, 1958.

Jenkins, Daniel. *Beyond Religion.* Naperville, Illinois: SCM Book Club, 1962.

Kenrick, Bruce. *Come Out the Wilderness.* New York: Harper & Row, 1967.

Knox, John. *Jesus: Lord and Christ.* New York: Harper & Brothers, 1958.

Lynn, Robert W. *Protestant Strategies in Education.* New York: Association Press, 1964.

McLendon, Jonathan C. *Teaching the Social Studies.* Department of Classroom Teachers, National Education Association, 1201 Sixteenth Street, N.W., Washington, D.C. 20036, 1960, 1963.

Meyerhoff, Hans, ed. *The Philosophy of History in Our Time.* Garden City: Doubleday (Anchor Books), 1959.

Michalson, Carl. *The Hinge of History.* New York: Charles Scribner's Sons, 1959.

Muilenburg, James. "The History of the Religion of Israel," in *The Interpreter's Bible,* Vol. I. Nashville: Abingdon Press, 1952.

Napier, B. Davie. *From Faith to Faith: Essays on Old Testament Literature.* New York: Harper & Brothers, 1955.

Neill, Stephen, and Hans-Ruedi Weber, eds. *The Layman in Christian History.* Philadelphia: The Westminster Press, 1963.

Niebuhr, Reinhold. *Faith and History.* New York: Charles Scribner's Sons, 1949.

Niebuhr, Richard. *Christ and Culture.* New York: Harper & Brothers. Cloth, 1951; paper, 1956.

Niebuhr, Richard. *The Meaning of Revelation.* New York: The Macmillan Company. Cloth, 1946; paper, 1960.

Nielsen, Niels C., Jr. *God in Education: A New Opportunity for American Schools.* New York: Sheed and Ward, 1966.

Ogden, Schubert M. *Christ Without Myth.* New York: Harper & Brothers, 1961.

Perkins, Dexter, John L. Snell, *et al. The Education of Historians in the United States.* New York: McGraw-Hill Book Company, 1962.

Phenix, Philip H. *Education and the Worship of God.* Philadelphia: The Westminster Press, 1966.

Phenix, Philip H. *Realms of Meaning: A Philosophy of the Curriculum for General Education.* New York: McGraw-Hill Book Company, 1964.

*Religion in the Public Schools*, a Report of the American Association of School Administrators. New York: Harper Chapel Books, 1964.

Richardson, Alan. *History: Sacred and Profane*. Philadelphia: The Westminster Press, 1964.

Riesman, David, with Nathan Glazer and Reuel Denney. *The Lonely Crowd*. New Haven: Yale University Press. Cloth, 1950; paper, 1960.

Robinson, Theodore H. "The History of Israel," in *The Interpreter's Bible*, Vol. I. Nashville: Abingdon Press, 1952.

Rogers, Edward. *Poverty on a Small Planet*. New York: The Macmillan Company, 1965.

Shiner, Larry. *The Secularization of History: An Introduction to the Theology of Friedrich Gogarten*. Nashville: Abingdon Press, 1966.

Shinn, Roger Lincoln. *Christianity and the Problem of History*. St. Louis: Bethany Press (Abbott Book), 1953, 1964.

Shotwell, James T. *An Introduction to the History of History*. New York: Columbia University Press, 1922.

Temple, William. *Nature, Man and God*. London: St. Martin's Press, 1934.

*The Cambridge Modern History*. A. W. Ward, G. W. Prothero, and Stanley Leathes, eds. New York: The Macmillan Company, 1907.

Tiegs, Ernest W., and Fay Adams. *Teaching the Social Studies: A Guide to Better Citizenship*. New York: Ginn and Company, 1959.

Tillich, Paul. *Systematic Theology*, Vol. I. Chicago: The University of Chicago Press, 1951.

Toynbee, Arnold J. *Civilization On Trial*. New York: Oxford University Press, 1948.

Troeltsch, Ernst. *The Social Teachings of The Christian Churches*, tr. Olive Wyon. New York: The Macmillan Company, 1931.

Van Leeuwen, Cornelius Th. *Christianity in World History*. London: Edinburgh House Press, 1964.

Walker, Williston. *A History of the Christian Church*, rev. ed. Edinburgh: T. & T. Clark, 1959; first published, 1919.

Walsh, W. H. *Philosophy of History: An Introduction*. New York: Harper Torchbooks, 1951, 1960.

Weatherhead, Leslie D. *The Will of God*. Nashville: Abingdon Press, 1944.

Wentz, Frederick K., ed. *My Job and My Faith*. Nashville: Abingdon Press, 1967.

Williams, Colin. *Faith in a Secular Age*. New York: Harper Chapel Books, 1966.

Wilmore, Gayraud S. *The Secular Relevance of the Church*. Philadelphia: The Westminster Press, 1962.

Winter, Gibson. *The New Creation as Metropolis*. New York: The Macmillan Company, 1963.

Wood, H. G., and others. *The Kingdom of God and History* (No. 3, Oxford Conference Books). New York: Harper & Brothers, 1938.

Woodward, C. Vann. *The Age of Reinterpretation*. Publication Number 35, Service Center for Teachers of History, 1961.

Wright, G. Ernest. "The Faith of Israel," in *The Interpreter's Bible*, Vol. I. Nashville: Abingdon Press, 1952.

Younger, George D. *The Church and Urban Power Structure*. Philadelphia: The Westminster Press, 1963.